NAMIBIA: THE ROAD TO SELF-GOVERNMENT

NAMIBIA: THE ROAD TO SELF-GOVERNMENT

JEFFREY B. GAYNER

Council on American Affairs
1716, New Hampshire Ave., N.W.
Washington, D.C. 20009

This publication is one of a series of monographs produced by the Council on American Affairs in conjunction with the Council's quarterly *Journal of Social and Political Studies*. Other monographs include *China — The Turning Point; Korea in the World Today; South Africa — The Vital Link; Rhodesia Alone; Sub-Saharan Africa: An Introduction; Sino-Soviet Intervention in Africa; The Panama Canal in Perspective; Constitutional Limits to Union Power; Trade Unions and Labor Relations in the U.S.S.R.; American Labor Unions: Political Values and Financial Structure;* and *Saving Social Security.*

ABOUT THE AUTHOR

Jeffrey B. Gayner is Director of Foreign Policy Studies for The Heritage Foundation. He is contributing author to *South Africa — The Vital Link*, editor of *Trial in Africa — The Failure of U.S. Policy*, co-author of *Allende and the Failure of Marxism in Chile*, and contributing author to five other books. His articles have appeared in *Policy Review*, the *Intercollegiate Review*, the *Journal of International Relations*, the *Journal of Social and Political Studies* and *Asia Mail*.

Copyright by the Council on American Affairs 1979

CONTENTS

I. WEALTH IN THE WILDERNESS 5

II. THE PEOPLE OF NAMIBIA 11

III. A BRIEF HISTORY OF NAMIBIA 17

IV. THE WESTERN PLAN FOR NAMIBIA 23

V. THE PROBLEM OF THE WALVIS BAY 35

VI. SWAPO 40

VII. FROM THE WALDHEIM PLAN
TO THE PRETORIA SUMMIT 50

VIII. POLITICAL PARTIES AND
THE NAMIBIAN ELECTIONS 59

IX. SOUTH AFRICA, THE U.N. AND ELECTIONS 81

XI. NAMIBIA AND THE FUTURE OF
SOUTHERN AFRICA 95

Map of Africa showing strategic location of Namibia

CHAPTER I

WEALTH IN THE WILDERNESS

Namibia may some day be regarded as a major source of many vital minerals in the world. Although not possessing the magnitude of oil riches of the Saudi's, Namibia does have vast untapped resources spread over a huge, nearly unpopulated desert wasteland. Only a costly confrontation using the best equipment and substantial capital investment forces the land to yield up its bounty. Without such an effort, the small diverse population of the territory would continue to eke out a marginal existence in those very limited fertile regions that allow human habitation. Thus, not surprisingly, the area never attracted much attention until political controversies were supplemented with the new recognition of potential wealth. Only now does interest in the territory begin to match the degree of neglect and relatively benign colonization.

Located on the southwest coast of the African continent, Namibia sprawls over an area equal in size to ten European countries combined, or approximately 318,261 square miles. As indicated on the map below, the area is bounded on the north by Angola and on the east reaches Rhodesia through a narrow strip of land that divides Zambia and Botswana. The shared border with South Africa has served as the principal overland route of contact and commerce with the rest of the world as politics in recent years has restrained relations with both Angola to the north and Botswana to the east. The Tropic of Capricorn bisects the area almost in half.

Only in 1968 did the name Namibia become affixed the area when the United Nations began using this term to refer to what had long been known as South West Africa, often written SWA. The area has in the past existed under a long series of names. As one commentator noted:

The history of SWA/Namibia is as intriguing and unique as the names that have been given to it in the past: 'no man's land', 'the land between the Crosses', Transgariep, Great Namaqualand, Damaraland, Hereroland, Ovamboland, the German West Africa 'Schutzgebiet', the South West Africa Protectorate, the South West Africa Mandate Territory. (1)

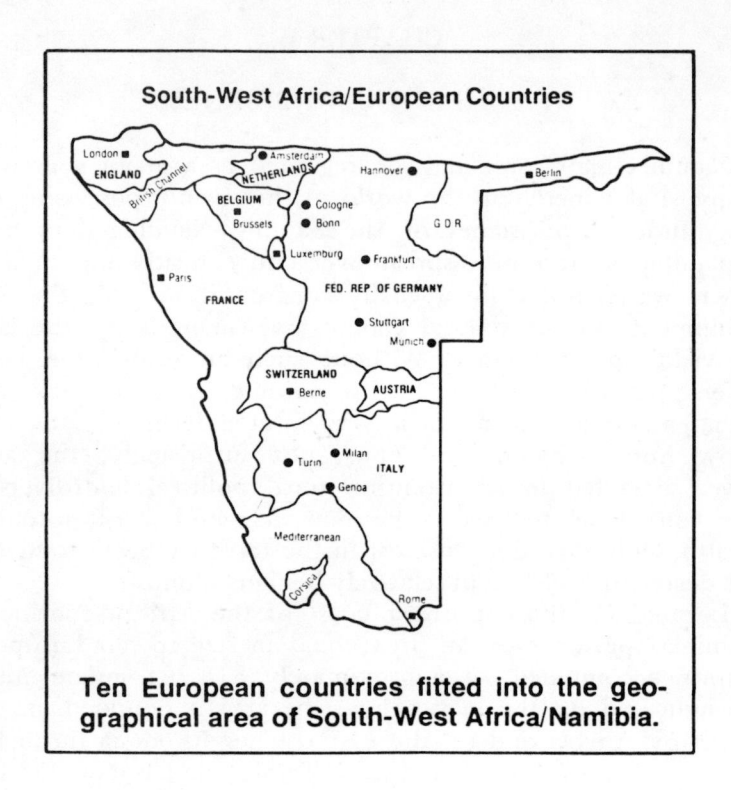

Ten European countries fitted into the geographical area of South-West Africa/Namibia.

Most of the area is probably best described by the phrase 'no man's land.' Of the three topographical regions of Namibia, only the northern area is suitable for any significant agricultural use. As the chart below dealing with rainfall indicates, most of the area suffers from perpetual drought conditions. Only with the creation of several dams did some parts of Namibia become habitable and a slightly larger portion of the area usable for farming. Nonetheless, as another chart demonstrates, real cropping potential still only exists along the narrow strip of land across the northern border of the territory. Neither the central plateau area nor the great Kalahari desert of the south area are suitable for anything but mineral excavation.

To compound the problems of the terrain further, what little rainfall exists generally appears erratically with the long seasons of absolute dryness followed by torrential downpours for short periods. This both prevents even minimal cropping and also means the absence of any permanent inland rivers.

WEALTH IN THE WILDERNESS 7

Thus all inland transportation must be overland. The only large river runs along the borders of Namibia, with the Kunene and the Okavango Rivers being used to provide some source of irrigation.

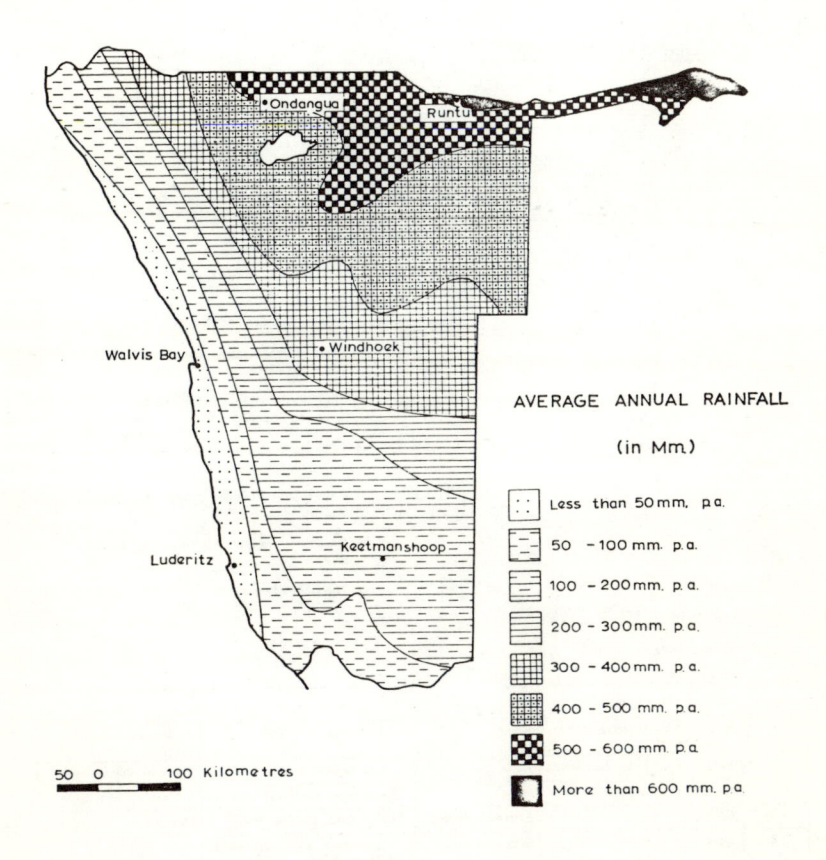

AVERAGE ANNUAL RAINFALL

(in Mm.)

- Less than 50 mm. p.a.
- 50 – 100 mm. p.a.
- 100 – 200 mm. p.a.
- 200 – 300 mm. p.a.
- 300 – 400 mm. p.a.
- 400 – 500 mm. p.a.
- 500 – 600 mm. p.a.
- More than 600 mm. p.a.

Agriculture remains of necessity very limited because nearly 70% of the land precludes any such use. Moreover, only a little more than 1 percent of the land can be used for normal agricultural dry land farming. Thus the principal agricultural pursuit consists of livestock grazing with often enormous areas needed to sustain the animals. The limitations upon the land are summarized in the following map and table:

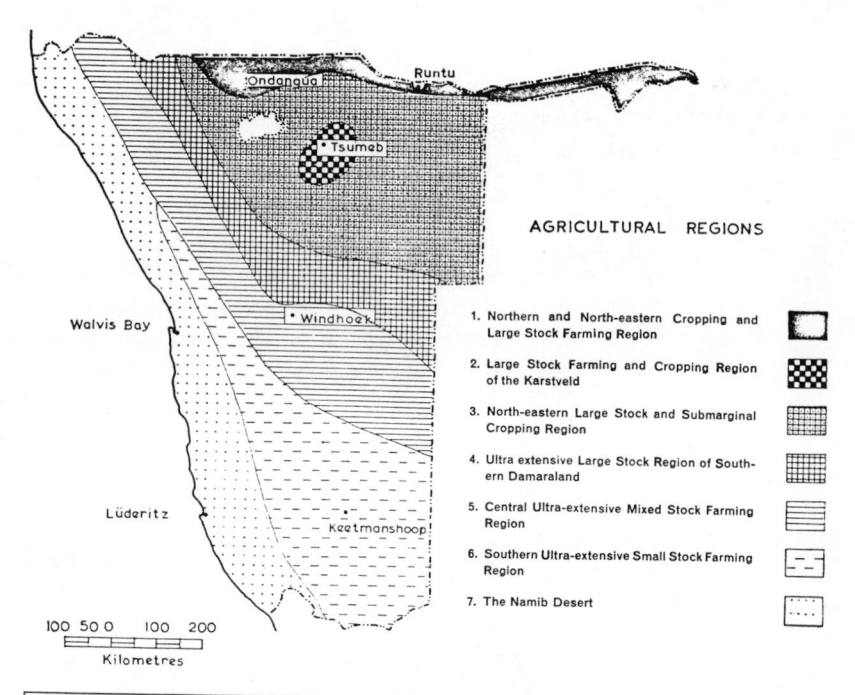

AGRICULTURAL REGIONS

1. Northern and North-eastern Cropping and Large Stock Farming Region
2. Large Stock Farming and Cropping Region of the Karstveld
3. North-eastern Large Stock and Submarginal Cropping Region
4. Ultra extensive Large Stock Region of Southern Damaraland
5. Central Ultra-extensive Mixed Stock Farming Region
6. Southern Ultra-extensive Small Stock Farming Region
7. The Namib Desert

Region	Dry-land Cropping[1]	Irrigation	Stock Farming[2]	Timber
1	Normal to marginal; soil fertility low to moderate	Good	Large stock, extensive	Extensively exploitable
2	Marginal; soil fertility moderate	None	Large stock, extensive	Some exploitation possible
3	Submarginal; soil fertility low	None	Large stock, extensive	Extensively exploitable
4	None	Extremely limited	Large stock, ultra-extensive	Negligible
5	None	Extremely limited	Large stock, and small stock, ultra-extensive	None
6	None	Limited	Small stock, ultra-extensive to marginal	None
7	None	Extremely limited	Marginal small stock farming in better parts	None

The only manner in which the land can be more efficiently used than at present would require still larger infusions of investment, particularly in irrigation projects in the north. As long as political instability exists in that same area it seems unlikely that what little potential exists for further agricultural development will take place.

Despite the natural drawbacks of the land, substantial development of the territory took place under the auspices of first the German colonists, who developed much of the limited agriculture, and later the South Africans. For over 60 years Pretoria subsidized the economy of Namibia; in 1977/78 this amounted to $70 million. Beyond subsidies South Africa lost $18 million operating the railroads, post offices and broadcasting services. Particularly since the end of World War II, South Africa has provided the loans needed to develop the basic infrastructure of the area, including transportation, health, education, postal and communication services upon which any modern economy must rely. Largely through these efforts the territory has realized real growth of over 5 percent per annum for the past 15 years. Overall 80 percent of all goods produced in Namibia are exported while about half of the goods and services used for local consumption are imported. In 1977 it was estimated that if Namibia had been an independent country that it would have shown a trade surplus.

Until the last few years the main products for export from the area consisted of a large but declining fishing industry, and some livestock and pelts. Fish products (fresh and canned fish, fish oil and fish meal) still have an annual export value of about $75 million while Karakul sheep pelts and livestock products raise an additional $160 million. Only with recognition of mineral wealth in the past decade did the prospects of real prosperity strike Namibia.

In 1977 Namibia exported minerals worth upwards of $200 million, consisting of diamonds, copper, vanadium, lead and zinc. This makes Namibia the fourth largest African mineral exporter, following South Africa, Zaire and Zambia. The value of exported gemstones also surpassed $200 million in 1977. In response to a Congressional inquiry, the U.S. Department of Commerce provided the following estimate of present and potential mineral development in Namibia:

Copper reserves are estimated at two million metric

tons with annual output totaling about 32,000 metric tons. Diamonds reserves total about five percent of the total world reserves of diamonds. Annual production is approximately 1.5 million carats of gem diamonds and 80,000 carats of industrial diamonds. Silver reserves are 15 million troy ounces, and production is estimated at 1.5 million troy ounces annually. Zinc reserves are about 300,000 metric tons with annual output reaching 40,000 metric tons. There are no statistics on the production of uranium, but it is estimated that Namibia has about five percent of the total world reserves of that mineral. (2)

The largest boom in wealth has derived from uranium. The British company, Rio Tinto Zinc (RTZ), has invested $120 million pounds ($240 million) in the Rossing Uranium Mine which will eventually be the largest such mine in the world. In 1977, operating at only three-fifths capacity (or 3042 short tons of production), it earned $175 million in foreign exchange and already surpasses RTZ's uranium production in Canada. Total uranium reserves at Rossing have been estimated at over 300 million tons. Estimates place earnings in the past year for all uranium production at $255 million and possibly rising as high as $2 billion in another decade as both production and the price of uranium rise. (3)

Some satellite photos indicate a large amphibolite belt full of uranium copper, and other minerals extending along the coastal area. Gas has been discovered near the port of Luderitz and some surveys reveal good prospects of some offshore oil.

This potential wealth, especially in a world of increasing mineral scarcity, should give considerable concern about the future development of the resources of Namibia and their strategic accessibility.

FOOTNOTES

(1) D. S. Prinsloo, "SWA/Namibia: Towards a Negotiated Settlement," Foreign Affairs Association Study Report (August, 1977), p. 6.

(2) "Resources in Namibia: Implications for U.S. Policy," Hearings before the Subcommittee on International Resources, Food and Energy, of the Committee on International Relations, House of Representatives, June 10, 1975 and May 13, 1976, p. 164.

(3) "Namibia: It could stand on its own feet," *Economist*, August 12, 1978, pp. 75-76.

CHAPTER II

THE PEOPLE OF NAMIBIA

Fortunately Namibia has a population as small as the area is large, making it one of the most sparsely inhabited areas in the world. Aside from the few small cities, no significant concentrations of population exist by normal means of measurement. More people live along the northern border area than anywhere else, but even there mostly rural settlements dominate.

As with many other former colonies in Africa, what is now called Namibia embraces numerous population groups that have come together under one name only because of circumstances peculiar to the establishment of colonial borders. Thus, there is no such thing as a "Namibian" in the sense of a nationality group, like the French or Germans in Europe, who largely inhabit the terrain that bears their name.

Instead Namibia really describes a place just as the former geographical description, South West Africa did more simply. As with other African territories an attempt is now made to artificially imbue an area with nationalistic aspirations, where in reality tribal and other loyalties clearly dominate the population groups. This does not mean that the people of Namibia do not aspire to remove themselves from the embrace of the South African Government. In fact even the white population in the area supports independence. All of the groups in Namibia, for example, support the annexation of Walvis Bay into Namibia, allowing the practical value of that port to override South African legal justifications for remaining in control of that enclave even following independence for Namibia itself.

However, potentially severe problems exist in Namibia under any formula for independence because the people in the area share more a common history of overlordship than any common customs, traditions or aspirations. Whereas some have contended that South Africa has effectively exploited these divisions and thereby kept the territory intact longer than any former colonial preserve, others note that Namibia has prospered and been relatively free of internecine civil wars that have characterized other African nations. The fundamental question remains whether a day of division in the territory has been postponed, or whether the delay in acquiring an independent status may mean the creation of a durable, democratic representative government.

While the total population still consists of probably slightly under one million people, regional tribal and racial differences divide this total into at least a dozen different identifiable subgroups. The complications, and with them the potential conflicts, in Namibia are illustrated best by a brief survey of these diverse groups of people:

Ovambo: Certainly the largest and probably the most important group of people in Namibia, are the Ovambo, concentrated in the northern border area of the country. They have tribal links much closer to the Cuanhama tribe in southern Angola than to any other groups in Namibia derives from historical and tribal connections that bear no relationship to the actual border line.

The Ovambo make up about 45 percent of the population and thus prognosticators often cite this group as eventually dominating any future government in Namibia. But substantial divisions exist among the Ovambo who encompass eight different tribes: the Ndonga, Kuanyama, Kuambi, Ngandjera, Kualuthi, Mbalantu, Nkolonkati and Eunda. Each of these groups has its own territorial area of concentration within the larger area generally described as Ovamboland. Historically great rivalries between these groups has led to wars.

Whites: With only a little more than 100,000, the white European descendents make up the second largest population group in Namibia. These 12 percent of the people have dominated Namibia since the German colonization. Initial white settlement preceded the appearance of the Germans and eventually congregated in the few urban and industrial areas of the country. Much more of a German or Afrikaans background characterizes the white population than in South Africa which has a large English speaking population.

While 70 percent of the whites speak Afrikaans as their primary language, 23 percent speak German and only 7 percent English. As in South Africa and Rhodesia the families of many of the whites arrived in Namibia several generations ago and consequently they regard themselves as natives of the land just as much as the black and mixed racial groups.

Dama: The next largest group, the Dama, number about 75,000 or a little more than 8 percent of the people. The Dama apparently once existed as slaves of the Nama and permanently adopted their language. This group initially was spread out over much of the most remote areas of Namibia and only in 1870, when missionaries interceded on their behalf, did German administration set aside a section of Namibia, northwest of Windhoek near the coastal area, where the Dama have now developed their own local governing councils.

Herero: Like the Damas, the Hereros also once lived under the control of the Namas. Believed to originate in the area west of Lake Tanganyika, this offshoot of the speaking Bantu peoples migrated south into the area along the Namibia-Botswana border and spread throughout the territory. Primarily herdsmen, many of the Hereros naturally moved into the sparse grassland areas. The group is best characterized by their unusual dual matriarchal and patriarchal pattern. The importance placed upon dual ancestry foster group ethnocentrism which mean a general distrust for all non-Herero people. The Herero speak a distinct variant of the Bantu language. While now somewhat diverse, the Herero at one time, in the late 19th century, dominated most of what is now Namibia.

Namas or Hottentos: The Nama, better known popularly as the Hottentots, have always played a prominent role in the history of the area of Namibia. While now only numbering about 40,000, they once dominated both the Hereros and the Damas. Originally from East Africa, they proceeded with a westward migration to the Atlantic and down into what is now South Africa. They always led a nomadic, herdsman existence and exterminated or enslaved rival ethnic groups. Only a part of the general Nama population moved into Namibia. In the years of warfare the Namas, as well as the Damas and Hereros, all found their populations substantially reduced, one reason why the Ovambo numerically predominate in any census today. The chart below tracks the population changes for the four ethnic groups discussed above.

Kavango: The Kavango, similar in size to the Herero, also are divided into other district sub-groups with five different tribes: the Kuangari, Bunja, Sambiu, Djirku and Mbukushu. These

Group[1]	1874/1876	1912	1928	1960	1966
Ovambo	98,000 (1876)		147,600	239,363	270,000
Herero	90,000 (1874)	19,721		35,354	40,000
Dama	20,000 (1874)	19,581		44,353	50,200
Nama	16,850 (1876)	14,320		34,805	39,400

1. This chart from *South West Africa Survey*, 1967.

tribes all live along the Okavango River and most speak the same Kuangali language. The Kavango reflect more of a pastoral existence with family villages and permanently occupied and cultivated land. The family remains the most important group with a matrilineal social system. Leadership of each of the five tribes is determined by an hereditary chiefdom.

Coloureds: Numbering only about 35,000, the Coloureds mostly migrated from South Africa and speak Afrikaans. As in South African they tend to concentrate in the cities and seek employment in the urban industrial and service sectors of the economy. Many own their own businesses and apparently moved to Namibia seeking greater economic opportunities.

Rehoboth Basters: Like the coloureds, the Rehoboth Basters originate from mixed ancestry, primarily European and Nama and moved north from South Africa's Cape colony. They also speak Afrikaans as their language and, despite their numbering only about 20,000, figure prominently in Namibian society by holding many professional jobs. They concentrate in the Rehoboth area, and have a Chief and Councillor form of government maintaining their old patriarchal social values.

East Caprivi: Like the Ovambo, Herero and Kavango, the East Caprivi also descend from the Bantu, though not directly related to any of these tribal groups. The East Caprivi, as the name implies, reflect more a geographical accident in the creation of the Namibia, than any other group. They inhabit the eastern end of the so-called Caprivi strip of land that the Germans established to provide access to the Zambesi river for their colony. The narrow strip of land has little in common with the rest of Namibia and is physically separated by a large swampland in its western sector. Even this small group can be further divided and many of their tribal compatriots share bordering areas of the surrounding countries of Rhodesia, Zambia, Angola and Botswana.

The Bushmen: Another small group of people with the closest ties to the most ancient inhabitants of the general area are the Bushmen. Also Bantu descendents, the Bushmen continue a primitive form of nomadic existence built upon traditional hunting and a narrow family centered social existence. The group has continually diminished in size with South African and other pressures exerted upon them to adopt a more settled existence.

Tswana: The smallest of the groups normally identifiable, and designated a particular geographic location by the South African administrators of the area, are the Tswana. They mostly live in the general area east of the Rehoboths, with close ties to tribes in Botswana.

Others: Still smaller groups of indigenous tribes exist in the general area of Namibia, but comprise less than two percent of the entire population.

The table below indicates the relative size of the various population groups as broken down into the dozen most generally accepted categories. No independent confirmation exists of the precise size of any population group and thus all figures must remain tenative, based on estimates derived from South African censuses over the years. The table does reveal, however, a substantial increase in the small population of the territory.

Population Groups in Namibia

Population Group	1960[1] Number	1966[2] Number	1974[3] Number	Percentage
Ovambo	239,363	270,900	360,000	46.5
Whites	73,464	96,000	99,000	11.6
Damara	44,353	50,200	75,000	8.8
Herero	35,354	40,000	56,000	6.6
Nama	34,806	39,400	37,000	4.3
Kavango	27,871	31,500	56,000	6.6
Coloureds	12,708	15,400	32,000	3.8
East-Caprivians	15,840	17,900	29,000	3.4
Basters	11,257	13,700	19,000	2.2
Bushmen	11,762	13,300	26,000	3.0
Kaokolanders	9,234	10,500	7,000	0.8
Tswana and Others	9,992	11,300	20,000	2.4
Total	526,004	610,100	852,000	100.0

1. 1960 Official Census.
2. Bureau of Statistics, estimated figures.
3. Africa Institute.

The chart below of the homelands designed by South Africa for each of the population groups reveals their general location and the fact that so much of the territory remains largely uninhibited. The homelands policy was eventually dropped due to its general unacceptability both to many of the inhabitants of Namibia and also to the international community, which has been hostile to its inherent principles.

NAMIBIA: Homeland locations of tribes

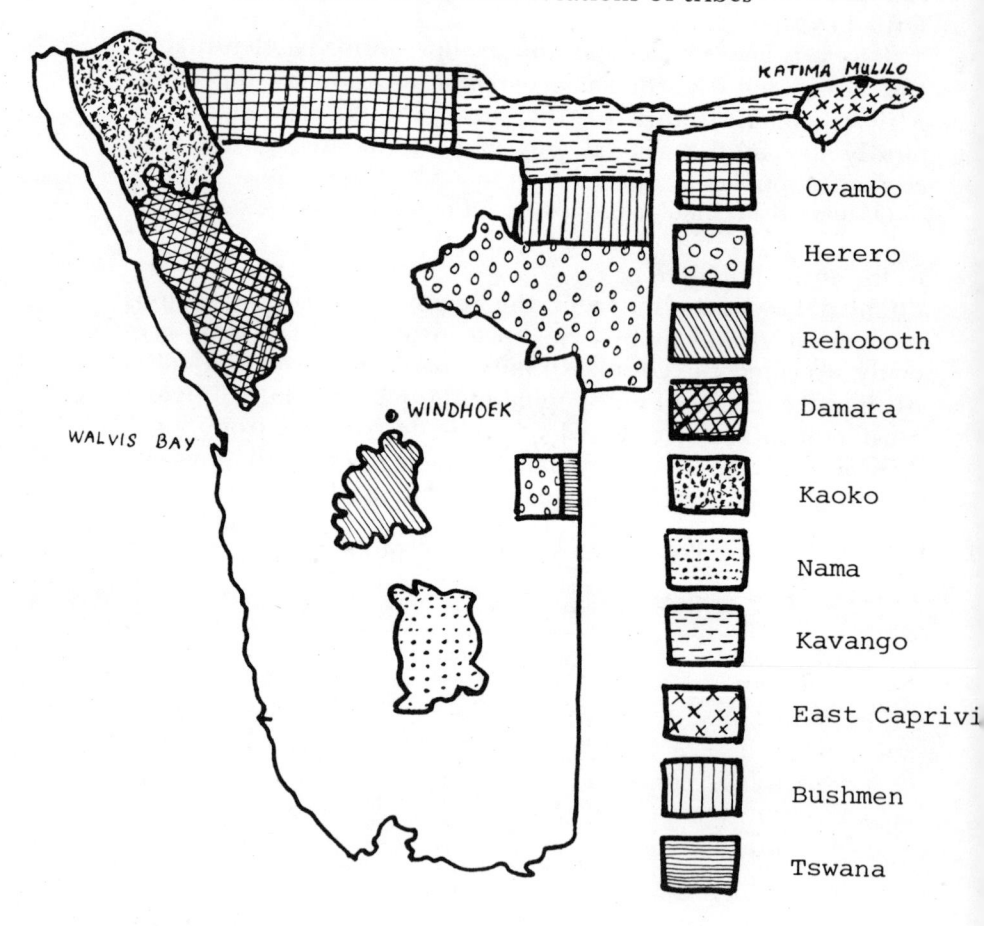

- Ovambo
- Herero
- Rehoboth
- Damara
- Kaoko
- Nama
- Kavango
- East Caprivi
- Bushmen
- Tswana

(Source: Africa Institute)

CHAPTER III

A BRIEF HISTORY OF NAMIBIA

European interest in southern Africa followed the establishment of a Dutch settlement at the Cape of Good Hope in 1652. Although the Portuguese travelled up and down the coast of Namibia for the next two hundred years, no significant development of the area took place until well into the nineteenth century. Not until 1878 did Britain annex various islands along the Namibian coast and in 1884 formally incorporated the Walvis Bay area into part of the Cape of Good Hope, primarily to avoid German annexation.

Just one year earlier the firm of F. A. Lüderitz of Bremen, Germany, purchased a large tract of land in southern Namibia from Nama Chief Josef Fredericks. The Germans acquired additional lands from local chiefs and proclaimed a protectorate over the area on October 28, 1884. Through agreements with Portugal in 1886, and Britain in 1890, German South West Africa extended over the area now known as Namibia.

The Germans remained in control of the area and settlers moved in for the next quarter century and firmly established their own cultural influence over the territory that still exists. By 1914 the white population reached 15,000. However, with the outbreak of World War I, South African forces easily captured the area in 1915 from the small 2,000 man German garrison. With the end of the war the Union of South Africa, created in 1910, formally took control of Namibia as a so-called "C" mandate under the league of Nations. Only President Wilson's general policy of "no annexations" prevented the complete incorporation of South West Africa as a part of the Union of South Africa. But the practical consequences of the "C" mandate status virtually amounted to annexation as South Africa oversaw all functions of the territory from 1915 to the present.

Legal Authority over South West Africa

The major controversy concerning the present status of the territory of Namibia derives from the confusion and conflicts over the precise nature of the mandates following the dissolution of the League of Nations in April, 1946. Under the mandate system South Africa was required to submit reports and account for her actions in Namibia to the Council of the League of Nations. The United Nations came into being in October 1945, six months prior to the official demise of the League. Through the creation of trusteeship arrangements the U.N. attempted to succeed to the authority the League had exercised under the mandate system. But no explicit provision existed for under the League for any transfer of authority from one organization to the other or under the U.N. Charter to assume such authority. Consequently South Africa asserted to the League in 1946 her intention to incorporate South West Africa when the mandate system came to an end. She then submitted this same proposal to the U.N. General Assembly which rejected it and recommended that the territory be placed under the Trusteeship System. South Africa then rejected this request and instead announced that she would continue to administer the territory under the previous mandate proposals.

South Africa clashed with the United Nations over this issue for the next twenty years with several major legal battles leading to a series of conflicting decisions before the International Court of Justice. In 1959 the ICJ ruled that the Mandate remained in force and the ICJ could oversee South African adherence to the mandate agreement. In 1960 the ICJ ruled 8-7 that it had jurisdiction, over South African objections, to settle disputes over Namibia, but at the same time a majority of the justices indicated that the U.N. had no right of succession to the League mandate. After finally taking up the case presented by Ethiopia and Libera in 1960 challenging South Africa's right to continue to rule Namibia, the ICJ in 1966 avoided the major issues, again ruling 8-7 that the two claimants had no legal right to question the performance of South Africa in fulfilling her legal obligations under the League mandate. Finally another advisory opinion by the ICJ in 1971, requested by the U.N. Security Council, declared that continued occupation by South Africa was illegal and that members of the U.N. should refuse to recognize the legal authority of South Africa in the territory. South Africa rejected this opinion as politically motivated by the United Nations.

A BRIEF HISTORY OF NAMIBIA

South African Administration of Namibia

From the time of the acquisition of her mandate over South West Africa, a large migration of South Africans took place so that by 1930 they outnumbered the German population in the territory. The strongly pro-South African United National South West African Party dominated local politics in the early years and the successor National Party later. The South West Africa Constitution Act conferred limited self-government on the territory in 1925. A quarter century later South Africa provided for an independently elected assembly in the territory which also sent representatives to the South African Parliament. However, South Africa still managed the principal administrative functions of the territory, including the police, armed forces, customs and immigration.

South Africa also attempted to transplant her social policies to Namibia. In 1962 the South African Government appointed a Commission of Enquiry into South West African Affairs, chaired by the late F.H. Odendaal. The Odendaal Commission issued a report two years later which recommended that the territory be divided into ten separate ethnic homelands, similar to the Bantustans in South Africa. These homeland divisions of the territory reflected the division made by the commission of the population into twelve separate ethnic groups. Major criticism of the plan centered on the allocation of 40 percent of the territory to homelands and 43 percent to the white population. Rehoboth Basters, the Coloureds and the government took the remaining lands.

South Africa attempted to implement the homelands policy for the next fifteen years. The Development of Self-Government for Native Nations in South West Africa Act in 1968 created six homelands, each with its own legislative and executive councils, although the State President of South Africa still retained ultimate authority. The South African Affairs Act of 1969 further consolidated power over the territory by Pretoria and attempted to make laws of Namibia conform to laws in South Africa.

U.N. Pressures Against South Africa

But while South Africa attempted to create ethnic federalism in South West Africa, international pressure mounted against her actions. With the failure of Ethiopia and Liberia to win their case in the ICJ, the United Nations decided to take international law into its own hands. Thus several months after the adverse decision, the U.N. General Assembly adopted a resolution, by a vote of 114 to 2 with 3 abstentions, that terminated South Africa's mandate over South West Africa and asserted, despite the ICJ action, that the territory be placed under U.N. jurisdiction. In 1966 the U.N. proceeded to create the United Nations Council for South West Africa to administer the territory until independence was attained. This group, renamed the Council on Namibia the following year, has continued to oversee Namibia, although none of its members have ever been able to exercise actual jurisdiction over the territory. But the UN has provided substantial support to the Council to train civil servants, provide educational grants for study and other functions that have largely contributed to the ability of SWAPO to wage political and guerrilla warfare against South Africa. By 1969 the Security Council began threatening South Africa both to cease its implementation of its homelands policy in the territory and also to withdraw from Namibia. The U.N. urged its members to support the struggle of the people of Namibia against South Africa. In 1970 another U.N. Security Council resolution declared that "all acts taken by the Government of South Africa on behalf of or concerning Namibia after the termination of the Mandate are illegal and invalid." (1) Following the favorable ICJ ruling in 1971 additional U.N. action hinted that sanctions should be imposed on South Africa for allegedly threatening the peace of the region by failing to withdraw from Namibia.

The U.N. Secretary-General visited both South Africa and Namibia in March, 1972, in order to pressure South Africa into granting independence to Namibia under U.N. auspices. In his report he charged that South Africa did not provide "the complete and unequivocal clarification of South Africa's policy in regard to self-determination and independence for Namibia envisaged in resolution 323 (1972)." (2) Following this meeting the Council on Namibia charged that the meeting had been counter-productive and, with later support from the Organization for African Unity and the Security Council, urged that no further discussions take place with South Africa.

The United Nations grew increasingly hostile to South

A BRIEF HISTORY OF NAMIBIA

Africa, even though Pretoria, as indicated below, began to substantially modify her policies towards Namibia. On December 12, 1973, the U.N. General Assembly decided to recognize the National Liberation Movement of Namibia, the South West Africa People's Organization, as the "sole and authentic representative of the Namibian nation. Two years later their view narrowed to recognize SWAPO as "the only and true representative of the Namibian nation."

The increasing hostility towards South Africa in the U.N. led to divisions among Western Nations over what course of action to pursue. In the 1973 vote on SWAPO, all five Western powers, who would later negotiate a settlement with South Africa, abstained. On two separate votes by the U.N. in May, 1975, and October, 1976, the U.S., Britain and France cast vetoes in the Security Council to prevent the imposition of a mandatory arms embargo against South Africa.

In the aftermath of the meetings with the U.N. Secretary-General in 1972 South Africa established a multi-racial advisory council from various ethnic, regional and other groups in South West Africa. Most significantly, South African Prime Minister John Vorster announced that his government would accept both the basic principles of independence and self-government in Namibia. Additional discussion eventually led the South West Africa Legislative Assembly to pass a resolution in November, 1974, calling for a broad multi-racial Constitutional Conference.

The Turnhalle Constitutional Conference, as it came to be called, opened in Windhoek September 1, 1975 with all eleven the population groups represented. As two of the leading authorities on Namibia have written in a recent study, the Turnhalle Conference

> was both an extraordinary success and a resounding failure. No matter what South Africa intended to do with the Turnhalle group, perhaps pull off a kind of U.D.I., *the conference politically awakened all segments of the population.* For the first time in the history of Southern Africa, *whites and nonwhites sat around a table* to discuss the peaceful devolution of white power. Each of the eleven major ethnic groups was represented by a separate delegation — whites, Bushmen, Coloureds, Herero. They were a most disparate collection; some highly sophisticated, some

at first quite ignorant concerning the workings of a modern government. The conference itself acted as an educative device; backwoods delegates, whose knowledge of modern administration has been negligible, turned into skilled negotiators wise in the minutiae of constitutional law. A strong collegiate spirit gradually developed. In order to maintain its cohesion, the conference operated on a principle never previously adopted by any constituent assembly in Africa: the principle of total consensus. Each delegate continued to argue his case until unanimity had been obtained on every key issue. (3)

The convention concluded its work by announcing December 31, 1978 as the prospective date of Namibian independence. They proposed the principle of a three-tier structure of government that would combine national and regional elements: the central government controlling national and state affairs would contain elements of all population groups; a second level of representatives of ethnic group would have wide latitude of action within their group; and finally cities and towns would create their own local governing mechanism. Both the central and second level governments reflected ethnic divisions of the country though at the same time a multi-racial governing council of ministers was established.

The proposal consisted of a hybrid of the original homelands policy and a democratic pluralistic society. This innovative approach to the problem of Namibia never completely materialized but formed a transition to the present government in Windhoek. In a referendum by white voters in May, 1977, 95 percent supported the proposed Turnhalle Constitution. But by this time South Africa had decided to enter into new negotiations with the Western nations in order to attempt to ensure international recognition for Namibia. Having already agreed both to abandon the homelands policy and also to grant independence to Namibia, Vorster decided to try to reach a reasonable accommodation if possible with his critics in the United Nations.

FOOTNOTES

(1) "Decolonization; Issue on Namibia," United Nations Department of Political Affairs, Trusteeship and Decolonization, No. 9, December 1977, p. 39.

(2) *Ibid.*, p. 40.

(3) Peter Duignan and L. H. Gann, *South West Africa-Namibia*, American African Affairs Association Inc., 1978, p. 25.

CHAPTER IV

THE WESTERN PLAN FOR NAMIBIA

With the U.N. threatening reprisals against South Africa in March, 1977, five Western nations (the U.S., Britain, Canada, Germany, and France) presented an aide-memoire to South Africa on April 7 which urged them to "facilitate the holding in Namibia on a territory-wide basis . . . free elections under the aegis of the U.N. and refrain from any steps inconsistent therewith." The five countries pressed for a settlement consistent with the U.N. resolution 385 in 1976.

In order to work out a detailed formula for the peaceful transition to a majority rule, independent nation status for Namibia the five Western nations sent senior representatives to South Africa at the end of April. South Africa did agree in principle to hold territory-wide elections in Namibia in order to elect a Constituent Assembly that would actually draft a new constitution. Following the meeting with South Africa, the five Western nations pursued further discussions with SWAPO, the United Nations Secretary-General, representatives from Tanzania, Zambia, Mozambique, Angola, Botswana and Nigeria as well as other political groups within Namibia.

Discussions continued for the next year in order to work out some precise formula agreeable to all of the conflicting parties in the Namibian dispute. The five Western nations met again with South Africa in Cape Town June 8-10, 1977; with SWAPO in New York August 8-11, 1977; with South Africa in Pretoria September 22-26; with SWAPO in New York October 14-19; and finished up the year with three weeks of meetings in Africa beginning on November 21, 1977, with President Nyerere of Tanzania, Foreign Minister Chissana of Mozambique, President Khama and Vice President Masire of Botswana, President Kaunda of Zambia, Prime Minister Do Nascimento and Foreign Minister Jorge of Angola, and Head of State Obasanjo of Nigeria.

Additional meetings in New York with SWAPO and South Africa led to the so-called proximity talks on February 11-12, 1978, between foreign ministers of the five Western nations, Foreign Minister Botha of South Africa and SWAPO President

Nujoma. By the end of March, the five Western nations proposed a draft agreement that was circulated as document S/12636 of the Security Council on April 10, 1978. This agreement provided for a framework leading both to implementation of U.N. Resolution 385 and the independence of Namibia. The agreement among the five Western nations on this plan constituted a "Proposal for a Settlement of the Namibian Situation" that still had to be approved by all of the parties in southern Africa.

Following the proposed draft agreement on April 10, the five Western nations sent representatives to South Africa to secure Pretoria's cooperation in carrying out the proposals. After several days of negotiations and discussions the South Africans formally agreed to the Western proposals on April 25. This agreement followed various clarifications to South Africa by the Western nations of the April 10 proposal. The entire April 10 proposal has been the source of major controversy over resolving the Namibia problem and will frequently be cited in this study. The basic provisions of the agreement South Africa assented to on April 25 all derive from the April 10 proposal. The principal provisions of the Western proposal consist of the following:

1. U.N. Special Representative: The U.N. Secretary General will appoint a Special Representative "whose central task will be to make sure that conditions are established which will allow free and fair elections and an impartial electoral process." (Section I, 2)

2. Cooperation with South Africa: "In carrying out his responsibilities the Special Representative will work together with the official appointed by South Africa (the Administrator-General) to ensure the orderly transition to independence." (Section I, 4)

3. Elections: "Elections will be held to select a Constituent Assembly which will adopt a Constitution for an independent Namibia." All adults will be eligible to vote by secret ballot. (Section II, 6)

4. Release of prisoners and return of refugees: "All Namibian political prisoners or political detainees held by the South African authorities" must be released prior to the electoral campaign. (Section II, 7B) At the same time "All Namibian refugees or Namibians detained or otherwise outside the territory of Namibia will be permitted to return" and also participate

in the elections. (Section II, 7C) "The Special Representative
. . . will ensure that Namibians remaining outside of Namibia
are given a free and voluntary choice whether to return."
(Section II, 7D)
5. Ceasefire and restrictions to bases: "A comprehensive cessation of all hostile acts shall be observed by all parties in order to ensure that the electoral process will be free from interference and intimidation." (Section II, 8) This entails "the restriction of South African and SWAPO armed forces to base." (Section II, 8A) In the twelve weeks following an effective ceasefire "all but 1500 South African troops" will be withdrawn from Namibia and these will be restricted to Grootfontein and Oshivello. (Section II, 8B) "SWAPO personnel outside of the territory (can) return peacefully to Namibia . . . to participate freely in the political process." (Section II, 8D)
6. Security functions: "Primary responsibility for maintaining law and order in Namibia during the transition period shall rest with the existing police forces." (Section II,9) During the transition period U.N. forces "commence monitoring of both South African and SWAPO troop restrictions." (Annex, point 3)
7. Border countries role: "Neighboring countries shall be requested to afford the necessary facilities to the U.N. Special Representative and all U.N. personnel to carry out their assigned functions and to facilitate such measures as may be desirable for ensuring tranquility in the border areas." (Section II, 12)
8. Timetable: The proposal is "designed to bring about a transition to independence during 1978." (Section I, 2) Independence for Namibia shall be "By 31 December 1978 at latest." (Annex, item 11)
9. Walvis Bay: Speaking to the U.N. on behalf of the five Western nations, Mr. Jamieson of Canada stated that "we have omitted from our proposal the difficult question of Walvis Bay for the reason that we see no way of settling the question in the context of the present negotiations."

On the day following the agreement with South Africa, United Nations Secretary General Kurt Waldheim acknowledged the progress made by the parties in a press release issued in New York. He noted that:
> the continued efforts that have been made by the five Western members of the Security Council over the past

year, have helped to establish a basis for a possible agreement within the framework of the Security Council resolution 385.

Yesterday's announcement by the Prime Minister of the Republic of South Africa that his Government accepts the Western proposals for a settlement is a positive step. The Secretary-General is in contact with the other parties and will comment on the substance of the South African statement after he has concluded his consultations.

Apparently the consultations did not prove particularly productive as the U.N. General Assembly proceeded with its Ninth Special Session on the "Question of Namibia." The session, begun on April 24th and concluded on May 3rd, adopted an extraordinary wide ranging 45 point "Declaration on Namibia" which completely failed to give any credit to the recently concluded negotiations. Instead the resolution criticized any role for South Africa in the determination of the future of Namibia, stating in point 18 that:

> The General Assemby rejects the idea that South Africa, as the illegal occupier of Namibia, has any legitimate interest in Namibia about which the South West Africa People's Organization should be pressed to make concessions in any negotiated and internationally acceptable settlement. South Africa has no right whatsoever to remain in Namibia or to procrastinate and prevaricate in any negotiating process on the question of genuine independence for Namibia.

Coming shortly after agreeing to the conclusion of procedures leading to democratic elections this indictment seemed particularly inappropriate. Beyond this the General Assembly also expressed:

> its full support for the armed liberation struggle of the Namibian people under the leadership of the South West Africa People's Organization, its sole and authentic representative. It expresses its conviction that the intensified armed liberation struggle by the Namibian people continues to be a decisive factor in the efforts to achieve self-determination, freedom and national independence in a united Namibia. (Point 14)

Rather than negotiation, the General Assembly called on its members "to render increased and sustained support and assistance to the South West Africa People's Organization to enable it to intensify its struggle for the liberation of Namibia." (Point 32)

The resolution (S-9/2) embodying these, as well as other points supporting all the positions of SWAPO in the Namibian dispute, was approved by the General Assembly in a vote of 119-0 with 21 abstentions. Conspicuous among the abstaining members were the five Western nations who had just negotiated the agreement with South Africa.

The South West Africa People's Organization initially rejected the Western nations plan and by its actions on May 3, 1978, the United Nations General Assembly reinforced this position. SWAPO instead called for an intensification of the armed struggle against South Africa as the best means of settling the future of Namibia. SWAPO representatives did agree, however, to meet and discuss the situation with representatives of the five Western nations.

These negotiations came to an abrupt halt on May 8 following a raid by South African forces against SWAPO bases located in the southern part of Angola. The South Africans sent a force of approximately 700 men over the border in a raid on May 5th in order to destroy base camps near Cassinga, Angola, used by SWAPO in conducting its guerrilla war against the people of Namibia. The South African Chief of Operations for the raid stated that his forces "came up against tough resistance, much stronger than we expected. SWAPO continued fighting to the last breath, so seriously that they were shot dead four deep in the trenches." (1) SWAPO leaders, on the other hand, claimed that most of the estimated 1,000 fatalities in the raid were civilian refugees.

The raid led to the suspension of further negotiations with SWAPO over Namibia and approval of still another resolution at the United Nations Security Council. The resolution, instigated by the Marxist government in Angola, demanded the "immediate and unconditional withdrawal" of South African forces from Angola and warned that any future attacks could lead to tough penalties such as trade sanctions.

A month later SWAPO issued a brochure entitled "Kassinga Massacre: Climax of Pretoria's All-out Campaign Against the Namibian Resistance." The publication, produced in East Germany, and distributed mostly in Europe and North America, contained photos allegedly proving that innocent civilian deaths resulted from the raids. Beyond that the piece also vigorously criticized the Western proposals on a settlement for Namibia.

SWAPO demanded changes in the Western plan which it said "cannot in its present form be regarded as final and definite." SWAPO claimed that the proposals "give South Africa extensive powers to control and influence the outcome of the transitional process to Namibia's independence." They charged that the five Western nations had "watered down" the U.N. resolution on Namibia, and insisted that:

> The fundamental flaw in these diplomatic efforts of the five has been the erroneous assumption that it was SWAPO that must be pressured, directly or through its friends, to accept to participate in elections which will merely be observed by the U.N. but which will in truth be controlled by South Africa. (2)

In particular SWAPO criticized the following elements of the plan: South Africa could retain her "entrenched administration" in Namibia during the transition, South African police forces would maintain law and order as well as 1,500 combat personnel, and finally, the West had not insisted on the transfer of Walvis Bay to Namibian control.

A summit meeting of five black African nations several days later led SWAPO into further negotiations with the Western nations. The five nations, led by Julius Nyerere, supported the basic objections SWAPO had raised and urged that negotiations with South Africa be reopened. This decision by SWAPO and the five African leaders came only a few days before South Africa, indicating its exasperation with SWAPO, decided to proceed with the plan agreed to in April.

Negotiations on an agreement with SWAPO continued for another month until a tenative course of action was reached on July 12, 1978. On that day a joint communique issued in Luanda, Angola, by representatives of the Five western nations and SWAPO, stated that during their discussions "certain points in the proposal of the five Powers were clarified and the two delegations accordingly agreed to proceed to the United Nations Security Council, thus opening the way to an early internationally acceptable settlement on the question of Namibia. (3) As subsequent discussion in the U.N. revealed,

SWAPO did not accept a detailed plan for a Namibian settlement such as South Africa, but instead simply agreed to proceed to the U.N. However, even the general SWAPO view differed significantly from the Western proposals, particularly including the introduction of the issue of the future disposition of Walvis Bay.

Thus on July 27, 1978, the U.N. Security Council again took up the Namibia problem and proceeded to pass two separate resolutions. The first resolution, adopted 13-0 with the Soviet Union and Czechoslovakia abstaining, contained only three provisions creating machinery for carrying out the Western plan. This provided that the Security Council:

1. Request the Secretary General to appoint a Special Representative for Namibia in order to insure the early independence of Namibia through free elections under the supervision and control of the United Nations;
2. Further request the Secretary General to submit at the earliest date a report containing his recommendations for the implementation of the proposal in accordance with the Security Council Resolution 385 (1976);
3. Urge all concerned to exert their best efforts towards the achievement of independence by Namibia at the earliest possible date.

The second resolution, dealing with Walvis Bay, passed by a unanimous 15-0 margin and nearly led to the withdrawal of South Africa from the entire agreement. This resolution and the entire question of Walvis Bay is examined in a separate chapter below. The attempt by the Security Council to include the disposition of Walvis Bay into the general settlement created the greatest initial controversy in the debate over U.N. actions on Namibia. Only after declaring her vigorous dissent to this second resolution, which had not been included in the April 25th plan, did South Africa reluctantly agree to proceed with the implementation of the first resolution.

Even on this first resolution, South Africa expressed grave reservations about many of the implications being drawn from general discussion of the framework the plan would eventually take. Although focusing initial attention on the Walvis Bay issue, the South Africans also raised objections to what they felt were serious deviations from the April 25 agreement they had reached with the five Western powers. In the weeks leading up to the eventual report the areas of potential disagreement appeared to be growing and thus the eventual rupture between South Africa and the Waldheim plan could easily be anticipated even before the precise details appeared. The areas of disagreement consisted of three major issues and several potentially troublesome problems.

The Role and Placement of the South African Armed Forces

Under the general settlement, South African armed forces would be reduced in number from their then estimated strength of about 25,000 men down to 1500, stationed in two bases in the northern part of the country where SWAPO forces are also concentrated. South Africa has emphasized the role of a general ceasefire preceding any military force reduction. Foreign Minister Botha, in his speech before the Security Council on July 27, noted that his government had "been influenced decisively by the provision that there should be a complete cessation of hostilities including, inter alia, minelaying, killings, abductions, etc., before any reduction in South African forces takes place."

While the general plan would allow South Africa to continue to have authority over her remaining troops in the territory, the U.N. military personnel would be stationed throughout Namibia. However, SWAPO's leader Sam Nujoma asserted a very different view by claiming that "The racist forces must be disarmed and placed under the direct command of the U.N. peacekeeping forces in one camp, the location of which will be decided by the Security Council." Naturally he also insisted that South African forces abandon Walvis Bay where South Africa believed other personnel, beyond the 1500 limit, could be stationed. In an interview in Madrid, SWAPO's deputy chairman Muyongo stated that after the election "our troops will guarantee territorial integrity including the port of Walvis Bay." Finally, Nujoma inverted the ceasefire formula by asserting that South African forces must be confined to bases before a ceasefire can be considered. Even then he talked ominously about the struggle continuing. (5)

The size of the U.N. and South African forces are integrally related to the effectiveness of a ceasefire. Initially, South Africa had proposed that her own force levels be reduced from over 20,000 down to 4,000 as the ceasefire and transition to independence progressed. However, the five Western nations persuaded South Africa that a comprehensive ceasefire could be implemented and on that basis the South Africans agreed to reduce their force levels to 1,500. At the time the Western nations indicated that U.N. forces would about equal South African forces or, mostly for psychological reasons, be slightly larger, or up to 2,500.

Upon the conclusion of a tentative agreement with SWAPO, the Western powers indicated that the U.N. force would consist of a military force of 5,000 men supplemented by perhaps 1,000 administrative personnel. This substantial increase in personnel led the South Africans to object that on the one hand, a ceasefire required so few of their personnel to remain in Namibia, but, on the other, such a large U.N. contingent was required. Moreover, the size of the U.N. force had profound psychological implications for South West Africa which believed that since the U.N. officially recognized SWAPO as the "sole legitimate and authentic representative of the Namibian people" that the larger the U.N. force the greater likelihood that any elections administered under its oversight would unfairly promote SWAPO. SWAPO tacitly reinforced this belief by insisting on a large U.N. contingent and the removal of all South African forces.

Elections: Timetable and Procedures

South Africa insisted that since the 1972 Turnhalle Convention Namibia should become independent by the end of 1978. In his speech to the Security Council, Botha bluntly warned against any delays in this timetable by stating "Our acceptance on April 25, 1978, was rested on the assumption that the proposal would be implemented in good faith by December 31, 1978 — not 'at the earliest possible date' if this phrase were to signify a later date."

Towards this end the South African government initiated a voter registration campaign following the April agreement. In September, South Africa extended for a month, to October 20, the deadline for registration. By early October, 90 percent of the population of the territory had been registered, although some church groups in Namibia complained that some people had done so only under duress. Nujomo, the head of SWAPO, disputed the validity of the registration campaign under South African auspices. The United Nations ostensibly supported Nujoma's position because one of the main reasons for delaying elections centered on establishing a verified voter role.

The timetable for elections thus became one of the principal points in dispute between the U.N. and South Africa. The July agreement proposed elections be held seven months after U.N. adoption of the U.N. plan for Namibia, which would mean holding elections no sooner than April, 1979. On the other hand, South Africa maintained that the seven months period agreed to by Western nations should date from the April proposal. Therefore Pretoria asserted that delays by other parties, namely SWAPO and the U.N., should not delay independence for Namibia. According to Botha, "the negotiations on the Western proposals have stretched over fifteen months. South Africa lent its full cooperation to these efforts." In contrast he argued that SWAPO's "intransigence was intended to delay the date of independence for the territory. These delaying tactics and statements raise doubts that they are willing to participate in genuine elections."

Administration of Namibia Prior to Independence

Another major disagreement between SWAPO and South Africa centered on authority in the territory during the period between a ceasefire and the installation of a new elected government. Nujoma argued in the Security Council that the United Nations special representative should outrank and be able to overrule the South African Administrator General. He maintained that the U.N. Council for Namibia was the only legal authority over the territory. In an interview Nujoma outlined his views further by maintaining that "the U.N. special representative will be responsible for security arrangements, law and order, taking the population census and the registration of voters. He will be responsible for announcing the results of the election." (6)

Most of the authority Nujoma attributed to the U.N. representatives the South Africans maintained should reside in the present Administrator General, Justice Steyn. In an interview, former Prime Minister Vorster insisted that "it must be understood very clearly that the special representative of the secretary general is not a dictator in South-West Africa, and he doesn't come to South-West Africa as a dictator. He comes there to work in close conjunction with the administrator-general, who is not only in charge of the election but who, in accordance with the understanding and the agreement, is also running the territory until such time as it becomes independent." (7)

Summary of Problems:
The problems anticipated in the wake of the July Security Council meeting and U.N. resolutions on Namibia were summed up very well by *To the Point* magazine which noted that "the whole project is now crawling with contradictions and dire threats. They include:
* The ceasefire. South Africa's belief that a *ceasefire* must precede anything else *is contested by Nujoma*, who says SWAPO will not stop fighting until all South African troops are confined to their bases.
* The size of the UN forces. Waldheim says he is planning to send 5,000 troops and 1,000 civilians. SA says the figure is too high for a situation of ceasefire and that *anyway the Western plan provides for the numbers to be determined in consultation with it.*
* The role of the secretary-general's representative. The resolution provides for him to supervise and control the whole process to independence. *Nujoma says he must initiate all processes*. And Vorster says his function will merely be to ensure the fairness and appropriateness of steps taken by the South African administrator-general in the territory Justice Marthinus Steyn.
* Walvis Bay and political prisoners. Again, Nujoma says the former must be handed over and the latter released before his men stop fighting. Pretoria says the plan provides for the reverse procedure.
* The election process. Steyn has already begun the registration of voters *(more that 60 percent have so far registered)*. Nujomas says no move must be made until the UN takes over.
* Law and order. The plan provides for the existing police force to have the "primary responsibility" in this sphere, and for them to be *under the control of the administrator general*, but Nujoma wants Ahtisaari to take over. (8)

Ambassador Ahtisaari travelled to Namibia on August 7 and began his assessment and consultation with Justice Marthinus Steyn, the Administrator-General of the territory, appointed by the South African Government. Ahtisaari stated in August, while in Namibia, that his report would be "a public document available to everyone" and that the South African government would be given ample time to study it.

He remained in Namibia for seventeen days holding discussions with leaders of all of the various factions in the territory. He travelled over 10,000 kilometers throughout the country, often accompanied by Justice Steyn. On his departure from Namibia on August 23rd, Ahtisaari stated that he was "particularly heartened by the fact that all the parties I contacted acknowledged the cardinal importance of our mandate within the context of the Security Council resolution." He went on to indicate that "It is no secret that the key issues raised at my meetings with political parties relate to the current registration of voters, the date of the elections and independence, as well as the overall time-table for a settlement of the Namibian situation." On his return to New York, he stated that during his mission "The greatest problem . . . was the suspicions and doubts that have been created . . . I think, during these two and a half weeks, we were able to dispense some of the rather unreasonable doubts about the UN's impartiality and so on." (9)

While the vagueness of the initial U.N. proposal managed to allow all parties to interpret it in their own most convenient way, the subsequent report designed to carry out the plan could no longer mask the differences. For a period of nearly six weeks speculation and disagreements (indicated above) about the final nature of the U.N. Plan continued by both sides.

FOOTNOTES

(1) *Washington Post*, May 9, 1978, p. 1.
(2) *Washington Post*, June 9, 1978, p. 1.
(3) U.N. Document S/12775.
(4) *To the Point*, July 21, 1978, p. 9.
(5) Foreign Broadcast Information Service (cited hereafter as FBIS), August 16, 1978, E3; July 14, 1978, E1 and E5.
(6) *To the Point*, July 21, 1978, p. 9.
(7) *FBIS*, August 3, 1978, p. E12.
(8) *To the Point*, July 21, 1978.
(9) U.N. Press Release, August 23, 1978; August 25, 1978.

CHAPTER V

THE PROBLEM OF WALVIS BAY

Walvis Bay is a South African enclave on the Namibia coast. While consisting of only 420 square miles (or less than 1/10 of one percent of the total size of Namibia), the Bay is the only deep water port on the coast of southeastern Africa from Cape Town to Luanda. The Bay area is naturally protected by a 10 kilometer long sand spit. The main railroad terminus of Namibia is located in Walvis Bay with lines coming from Swakopmunc, Tsumeb and Grootfentein to the north and Windhoek in the east. Overall, 90 percent of Namibia's export trade passes through the Bay, including nearly all minerals.

South Africa has continually enlarged and diversified functions at Walvis Bay. It now consists of eight deep water berths, large fish-processing plants, coastal marsh lands and, like most of Namibia, huge shifting sand dunes. In contrast to Namibia, of the total permanent population of 26,000 in Walvis Bay, about 10,000 are white, most Afrikaners. Thus about 40 percent of the population of Walvis Bay is white compared to only 10 percent of the population of Namibia itself.

Historically, the British formally annexed Walvis Bay in 1878 shortly before the Germans annexed the rest of South-West Africa. In their proclamation at the time, the British made Walvis Bay a "part of the Colony of the Cape of Good Hope, and subject to the laws in force therein." A dozen islands off the coast also came under British jurisdiction and were also made part of the area that would later become South Africa.

When South Africa assumed her mandate over South West Africa in 1920, she proceeded to administer Walvis Bay and the islands as part of the annexed area while restating the fact that Walvis Bay was a part of the Cape of Good Hope. The Walvis Bay Administration Proclamation of 1922 provided that ". . . the port and settlement of Walvis Bay, which forms part of the Province of the Cape of Good Hope, shall be administered *as if* it were part of the mandated territory." This administrative convenience has led to great legal misunderstandings. The language of this proclamation parallels the controversial language in the 1903 Panama Canal treaty in which Article III grants authority "the United States would possess and exercise *if it were* the sovereign of the territory. . . ." In both situations the use of 'if' is descriptive rather than designating a formal change of de jure status.

In 1977, as Namibia began moving toward independence, South Africa issued a proclamation which declared that "Walvis Bay shall cease to be administered as if it were part of the territory and as if inhabitants thereof were inhabitants of the territory and shall again be administered as part of the province (of the Cape of Good Hope)." This proclamation led some nations and SWAPO to denounce what they described as the "annexation" of Walvis Bay by South Africa. The Front-Line states (Angola, Botswana, Mozambique, Tanzania and Zambia) have referred to this as the "dismemberment" of Namibia.

In March 1978, the United Nations Council for Namibia held several meetings in Zambia and adopted the Lusaka Declaration which declared that the decision by South Africa to re-incorporate Walvis Bay.

is an act of aggression against the Namibian people and has been rejected by the United Nations as illegal, null and void. This illegal annexation of Walvis Bay is a deliberate attempt to deprive Namibia of its main port and vital economic avenue and retain a strategic military base in this part of Namibia. Walvis Bay is an integral part of Namibia with which it is inextricably linked by geographical, historical, cultural, economic and ethnic bonds. The existence of military bases of South Africa in Walvis Bay is a threat to the territorial integrity and national security of Namibia. (1)

Until the agreement with SWAPO on July 12 and the subsequent resolution quoted, the Western nations appeared to support the legal position of South Africa. At the time of the April 25 agreement with South Africa on Namibia, the Western nations declared that "All aspects of the question of Walvis Bay must be subjected to discussion between the South African Government and the elected government of Namibia." On November 4, 1977, the Western governments abstained from General Assembly Resolution 32/9D which declared that Walvis Bay was an integral part of Namibia. In the series of regular Background Notes published by the United States Department of State, the issue which details with Namibia asserts that Walvis Bay "is administered as part of South-West Africa but in terms of sovereignty is an integral part of the Cape of Good Hope Province of the Republic of South Africa." (2)

But the United States and the other four Western nations apparently abruptly changed their positions on Walvis Bay in order to draw SWAPO into an agreement. At the time of the basic agreement with SWAPO on a Namibian settlement, Sam Nujomo, the President of SWAPO, stated that he would not accept independence for South West Africa without the inclusion of Walvis Bay in the new state. In a midnight press conference Nujomo stated that he "is going to see to it that the Security Council treats Walvis Bay as an integral part of Namibia." (3)

The United Nations went along with SWAPO's conditions and on July 27, 1978, adoptedResolution 432 (1978) dealing with the issue of Walvis Bay. The complete resolution read as follows:

1. Declares that the territorial integrity and unity of Namibia must be assured through the reintegration of Walvis Bay within its territory;
2. Decides to lend its full support to the initiation of steps necessary to insure early reintegration of Walvis Bay into Namibia;
3. Declares that, pending the attainment of this objective, South Africa must not use Walvis Bay in any manner prejudicial to the independence of Namibia or the viability of its economy;
4. Decides to remain seized of the matter until Walvis Bay is fully reintegrated into Namibia.

Secretary of State Vance implicitly acknowledged that the Western nations had completely changed their position by allowing Walvis Bay to enter into the U.N. debate:

From the beginning of our efforts to assist in the achievement of independence by Namibia in accordance with Security Council Resolution 385, our governments have been conscious of the strongly held views by the parties concerned on the status of Walvis Bay. Since these opposing views appeared to be irreconcilable, the five governments decided to take the position that they would not include any provisions on this question in their proposal for a settlement of the Namibian situation. Consequently, the terms of the proposal which we submitted to the Security Council on April 10 contain no mention of Walvis Bay.

Although voting for the resolution on Walvis Bay (quoted above), Secretary Vance asserted that "This resolution does not prejudice the legal position of any party. It does not seek to coerce any party." At the same time, Vance emphasized the practical value of the integration of Walvis Bay, noting that "We recognize that there are arguments of a geographical, political, social, cultural and administrative nature which support the union of Walvis Bay with Namibia." But the language of the resolution categorically states "Namibia must" include "the reintegration of Walvis Bay." Thus, since Walvis Bay had never been a part of even the mandate territory, the U.N., with Western support, boldly demanded the relinquishment of part of South African territory.

On July 28, 1978, the South African Prime Minister, John Vorster, succinctly stated the position of his government on the U.N. actions as follows: "Walvis Bay is South African territory and no decision by the United Nations or any other body can deprive South Africa of it. In fact, only a decision by the South African Parliament can bring about change to the status and position of the territory of Walvis Bay." In an interview several days later Vorster referred to the joining of the resolutions on Walvis Bay and Namibian independence as indicating "they wanted to doublecross us." This bitterness towards the Western nations hindered other negotiations since the summer of 1978 with South Africa on other issues.

Beyond the historical and legal grounds for asserting its intention to retain control over Walvis Bay, South Africa has advanced its own various vital interests in maintaining the enclave. The port is the fifth largest in South Africa with tremendous commercial value. Through control of the surrounding area, South Africa has access for air traffic stopover rights that are now denied them by most black-ruled nations to the north. Continued control of the area will undoubtedly provide them with important leverage in dealing with a future government in Namibia.

The main principle asserted by supporters of integration of Walvis Bay into Namibia consists of the geographic proximity of the area and its value as a port. But at a time when territorial integrity is asserted so adamantly in Africa, this principle is expeditiously abandoned in the case of South African rights in Walvis Bay. The Angolan enclave of Cabinda, just up the coast from Namibia, shares a similar geographic separation, but the Cabinda liberation movement fails to elicit African or much international support. Numerous examples exist of nations controlling or owning non-continguous territories adjacent to other nations, such as Hong Kong, Macao, Northern Ireland, Berlin, Guantanamo Bay, and Gibraltar.

South Africa has always agreed to negotiate with any duly elected future government of Namibia questions relating to the use of Walvis Bay, but have usually qualified this by referring to "friendly" governments. Somewhat fearful that a Marxist government may come to power in Namibia, South Africa believes that continued use of Walvis Bay would deter guerrilla action taken against South Africa itself. More broadly, legitimate fear exists that Marxist control of this port could have profound strategic implications for the entire South Atlantic area.

One suggestion for resolving the dispute over Walvis Bay would consist of making it a semi-autonomous free port, like Hong Kong. (4) However no leading political figures support such a compromise solution. Quite likely the level of conflict in the future over Walvis Bay will be determined by who comes to power in Windhoek. By November 1978, the issue quickly became overshadowed by the larger question of Namibian independence. The problem undoubtedly will arise if any group coming to power in Namibia desires to press the issue against South Africa, particularly in the hostile environment of the United Nations.

FOOTNOTES

(1)   As quoted in "Objective: Justice," United Nations Office of Public Information, Vol. 10, No. 2, Summer, 1978, p. 43.
(2)   U.S. Department of State, December 1974, p. 1.
(3)   FBIS, July 14, 1978, p. E5; *To the Point*, July 21, 1978, p. 9.
(4)   See "Free Port Best Solution for Walvis Bay," *To the Point*, 28 July, 1978, p. 28.

CHAPTER VI

SWAPO

In all of the discussions and debates on the future of Namibia, the South West Africa People's Organization invariably figures more prominently than any other political groups associated with the territory. The history of South West Africa and the history of SWAPO mesh constantly as both reflect the cross currents of tribal loyalties, political divisions, and the basic contest for power in the territory after the eventual departure of South Africa.

The origins of SWAPO can be traced back to the Ovambo People's Congress founded by Ovambo workers in Cape Town in 1957. Although proclaiming itself a broadly based effort to bring all the various tribal and ethnic factions together, the organization never has effectively extricated itself from its Ovambo origins. But since the Ovambo comprise the largest identifiable population group in Namibia, an organization associated with them naturally assumes particular importance. At present about 90 percent of the members of SWAPO come from Ovambo backgrounds, although some leading Hereros initially joined the organization. Very few whites have ever been admitted to membership.

Two of the early founders and leaders of the organization remain prominent figures in Namibian politics: Herman Toivo ja Toivo and Andreaas Shipanga. In 1959 Toivo changed the name of the organization to the Ovambo People's Organization and was joined at that time by Sam Nujoma and Mburumba Kerina (who is half Herero and half Ovambo). They received assistance from the Liberal Party and Communist Party in South Africa. With the rise of personal, philosophical, and tribal differences that so frequently have plagued SWAPO and Namibia, the Herero broke off from the organization in 1959 to form the South West African National Union (SWANU) in Windhoek. In order to confront the appearance of the narrowing of the ethnic base of the party, the Ovambo People's Organization became the South West Africa People's Organization or SWAPO. But the broader name, intended to attract territory-wide base of support, never effectively changed the Ovambo structure of the party; but it undoubtedly assisted the organization in later obtaining international recognition as being representative of all people in Namibia. This assisted Kerina who since 1956 had attempted to argue on behalf of the people of Namibia before the United Nations. In the early years of SWAPO a form of collegial rule developed in the organization as Toivo remained in charge in Africa, Kerina in New York, and Shipanga, Nujoma and others operating in important, but subordinate roles.

During this formative period the group advocated nonviolence, but by 1962 the decision had apparently been made to begin a campaign of guerrilla warfare and sabotage in Namibia. Training facilities for SWAPO guerrillas were made available by the Soviet Union, China, Algeria, Ghana, and Tanzania. Of the initial leaders only Shipanga apparently embraced Marxism, but soon Soviet support for SWAPO acquired strong ideological tones among the members. Initial guerrilla activities began in Namibia in 1965, and, following the dismissal of the Namibian case before the International Court of Justice in July, 1966, SWAPO decided to step-up its campaign. In 1966 Toivo took personal leadership of the ill-fated guerrilla campaign in Namibia. The South African authorities easily overpowered this initial effort and captured Toivo who was convicted and sentenced to prison on Robben Island near Cape Town where he remains today.

Following the arrest of Toivo, Kerina had Sam Nujoma appointed as the first President of SWAPO; Toivo had been chairman of the group and some still recognize him as the real leader. By the time leadership passed to Nujoma, division increasingly characterized SWAPO with both external and internal splits developing, as two leading authorities on Namibia point out:

> SWAPO was not a single organization. It had the external wing which carried on the "war of national liberation," and the internal wing which involved itself in peaceful political activities. "SWAPO Internal" was less radical than the exile organization — to survive, organize, and hold meetings it had to be. A substantial part of SWAPO's internal strength derived from church members, workers, and intellectuals who looked to radical social reform, and sometimes to a "theology of liberation." Other less

sophisticated adherents proclaimed their allegiance to the party because they saw it as an anti-white body, and because a SWAPO label seems to indicate opposition to the status quo. "SWAPO Internal" was by no means united. It contained at least three factions — the Ovambo group in the north, a southern faction made up of moderates, and a younger radical group — the Youth League — which called for a militant revolutionary movement to take charge of Namibia.

"SWAPO External" was an equally divided body . . . its headquarters were in Lusaka, with additional offices in Luanda, New York, London, Zamalek-Cairo, Hydra (Algiers), and Dakar. "SWAPO External" was led by men who had left Namibia in the early 1960s; they clearly were away too long to know what was happening inside their country. A split between the external and internal wings seemed obvious, although it has been averted so far by the control exerted over the purse strings by the external group. The latter was recognized worldwide for its diplomatic and military struggles. Both wings of SWAPO refused to participate in the Turnhalle conference. But there were obvious disagreements between those who had to live under a South Africa-dominated Namibia and those who, from the outside, carried on a guerrilla war. "SWAPO Internal," for example, had belonged to the Namibia National Convention (NNC), but "SWAPO External" would not join the NNC, claiming it alone could speak for Namibia. Similarly, "SWAPO External" continued to oppose cooperation with South Africa in implementing the West's initiative, yet "SWAPO Internal" could not be happy with this intransigence. It could mean that Namibia would become independent without SWAPO. (1)

The divisions between external and internal SWAPO loyalists centered on tactics that could dislodge South Africa and rival indigenous forces, but did not represent any fundamental philosophical differences on the kind of society SWAPO intended to create in Namibia. Thus these differences, while noteworthy, have not been nearly as important as some other splits.

The most important of these divisions arose in "SWAPO external" in the early 1970s as contrasting lifestyles and objectives developed between various elements of the organization. Young activist members of SWAPO who had carried the brunt of the campaign against South Africa in the rugged terrain of northern Namibia increasingly felt alienated from the leadership of Nujoma comfortably headquartered in Lusaka, Zambia. Rather than participating directly in the often strenuous struggle against the powerful South Africans, they found that Nujoma and his closest associates stayed out of Namibia itself and instead preferred the friendly, and much safer, propaganda battlegrounds of press conferences and meetings in various foreign capitals. Moreover, the young turks of SWAPO believed that vast sums of money collected from beneficent Scandinavian governments, liberal church groups, the OAU, and the Soviet block largely financed the often opulent lifestyle of the leadership in Lusaka, with only minimal support finding its way into the effort in Namibia itself.

The growing rift in the guerrilla wing of SWAPO finally erupted in open conflict in March 1976 when many of the younger activist members, under the leadership of Andreas Shipanga, met in southern Zambia and itemized a list of grievances against the Nujoma hierarchy. They charged his leadership with nepotism, corruption, waste, inefficiency and, in general, a lack of principled devotion to the cause of Namibian independence. In order to press their points they demanded that a new party congress of SWAPO be held in which the entire organization could discuss and eventually vote on the merits of their criticisms and ultimately decide the direction SWAPO would take in the future. Nujoma rejected their proposed challenge to his integrity and authority. This precipitated an attempted march by Shipanga and nearly 1,000 supporters upon the headquarters of Nujoma in Lusaka. However, Nujoma prevailed upon President Kaunda of Zambia to intervene in his behalf and the Zambian army surrounded and disarmed the protestors, forcing them into a prison camp at Boroma. Under the guidance of Nujoma, Zambian authorities continued to arrest additional dissidents in SWAPO and similarly confined them to prison, allegedly granting "protective custody for their own safety."

Shipanga's wife escaped during the massive wave of arrests and attempted to seek a repudiation of the actions through the judiciary system in Zambia. However, as soon as the Zambian Supreme Court agreed that no substantive evidence existed to justify the arbitrary arrests and imprisonments, Nujoma arranged through Kaunda and Julius Nyerere to have his leading opponents transferred to other prisons in neighboring Tanzania, near the town of Dodoma, where they remained until the spring of 1978. Thus, as Julian Amery wrote, "As a result of disagreements over internal elections of their officers, over 1,000 SWAPO supporters" were "held in detention camps outside Namibia at the request of one faction of the SWAPO leadership. Twelve of the leading dissenters, including Andreas Shipanga . . . being imprisoned without trial in the Dodoma prison in Tanzania. This of course hardly bodes well for the fate of democracy in Namibia." (2)

For nearly two years a campaign continued to secure the release of this large number of SWAPO dissidents. Details of the arrests and imprisonments were presented to major humanitarian organizations, such as Amnesty International, the International Commission of Jurists, the World Council of Churches, the United Nations, and the Scandinavian nations which had provided substantial funds for SWAPO. But, aside from some of the Scandinavians, none of these organizations pressed the issue of repression of dissent in SWAPO, but instead supported other efforts against South Africa to release far fewer SWAPO supporters imprisoned by the South Africans for waging guerrilla war in Namibia.

Somewhat sensitive to the criticism leveled against them, SWAPO created its own commission of inquiry into the problem of the dissidents. Not surprisingly, the report on discontent issued in December, 1976, reached the peculiar conclusion that because Shipanga remained opposed to violence he represented a threat to overthrow the leadership of SWAPO and therefore it was proper to arrest and detain him.

When questioned about the large number of political prisoners being held, SWAPO's European representative, Peter Katjaivi, asserted that members of SWAPO held by South Africa should not be confused with "internal SWAPO issues where SWAPO members were detained for disciplinary action."

The effort to secure the release of the SWAPO dissidents finally yielded results in May, 1978. Earlier in the year the Swedish Foreign Minister, Karin Soder, made a trip through

South Africa visiting most of the Front Line states who supported Nujoma. He specifically pressed the point of the incongruity of these nations promoting democratic rights in Namibia, yet maintaining Namibian political prisoners in their own countries. The five Western nations, having concluded an agreement in April with South Africa to hold free elections in Namibia, also raised the issue with the front line states. Thus, in May, Tanzania finally relented to the pressures and at least agreed to release nineteen key SWAPO dissidents, including Shipanga. Sweden consented to grant them political asylum.

Nujoma protested vigorously against the release of his opponents and demanded that they be sent to him rather than deported. But, unable to prevent release of the SWAPO dissidents, the Central Committee of SWAPO attempted to discredit them by repeating old charges of disloyalty against them. In a meeting on June 9 in Lusaka, SWAPO officially expelled eleven of those released, accusing them of having "organized and led a counterrevolutionary plot to sabotage the liberation struggle." Moreover, they were accused of acting "in collusion with certain imperialist Western countries to sabotage the political and military struggle of the Namibian people against the illegal South African regime" and of having planned "to assassinate a number of SWAPO leaders and comrades." (3)

In a press conference on August 26, Shipanga claimed that SWAPO still held 1,800 Namibians in prison in Zambia and that a "sinister plot" existed to prevent their return to Namibia. He requested Ahtisaari to secure their release from Zambia. (4)

How many additional SWAPO dissidents are imprisoned elsewhere is unknown. On August 9, 1978, SWAPO's secretary for publicity and information said, "SWAPO has released 11 counter-revolutionaries and we hold no more prisoners. Reports of thousands of prisoners still held by SWAPO are completely unfounded and we challenge anyone to prove the contrary." (5)

However, with no access to prisons in Angola, Zambia, or Tanzania, it was impossible to know just how many dissidents remain in custody. In the raid into southern Angola to destroy guerrilla bases on May 5, 1978, South African forces claimed that many people at the camps had been kidnapped or were otherwise being held against their will.

This major division in the ranks of SWAPO encouraged still

further strife and disaffection from Nujoma. A significant number of former leaders of SWAPO, including even Kerina, one of the co-founders of the organization, returned to Namibia in order to work for a peaceful formula for transition to independence. As noted below, Shipanga eventually returned to Namibia and, along with other dissenters from Nujoma's leadership, formed SWAPO-Democrats as a new political party.

Finally, tribal subdivisions among the Ovambo people also further ruptured SWAPO's earlier unity. The war in neighboring Angola had forced the various factions of the Ovambo people concentrated on the border, to choose sides in the conflict between the MPLA and UNITA. While UNITA shared much closer ethnic roots with the Ovambo, Nujoma sided with the Marxist oriented MPLA and aligned most of SWAPO against UNITA. However, the Kuanyama segment of the Ovambo sided with UNITA in the struggle and the Ovambo division still continues as does the fighting in Angola. With large numbers of Cubans and East Germans in Angola carrying the war against UNITA in 1978, Nujoma's alliance with the MPLA has considerably lessened his credibility as an African nationalist.

Although it is difficult to judge, most analysts estimate that Nujoma still commands the support of most of the Ovambo people. However, both the growing divisions within SWAPO over recent years, Nujoma's continued operations outside the country, and the active campaigns of other political groups for the allegiance of this major population group, increasingly indicates the outcome of any genuinely free election unpredictable. In the December elections held under the auspices of the South Africans, a surprisingly large turnout in Ovamboland indicated that the SWAPO campaign to intimidate voters from appearing at the polls failed. A U.N. presence substituted for a South African presence in a future election probably will not yield the kind of results that Nujoma has always anticipated.

The divisions within SWAPO resemble in some respects the divisions within the Patriotic Front in Rhodesia. But Nujoma has already consolidated political power by ruthlessly suppressing dissent within SWAPO just as it appears that Mugabe would attempt to do should the Patriotic Front come to power. While Nkomo still vies with Mugabe for leadership of the Patriotic Front, Shipanga and others can only challenge Nujoma in elections in Namibia overseen by a third party. Under a genuinely democratic framework, Ovambo opponents of Nujoma may be able to challenge his position effectively which they have been unable to do within the narrow SWAPO political framework.

SWAPO: Philosophy and Views

As indicated above, SWAPO initially developed as a nationalist movement for the liberation of Namibia. However, in its earliest stages a strong Marxist influence overcame the organization and by the late 1960s the principal leaders of the group used a Marxist lexicon in their denounciations of the South African and other alleged imperialists in Africa. Training and support by Communist countries reinforced a benevolent view of Communism. Nujoma increasingly structured SWAPO as a mirror image of a dictatorship of the proletariat political organization, with strongly centralized leadership and control.

Nonetheless, in most of its official statements and general public posture, SWAPO continues to insist that it merely represents a "popular movement" much as other groups in Africa have proclaimed themselves to be. However, its party program has now almost completely embraced a Marxian view of the world. In July, 1976, SWAPO revised its constitution and adopted a revealing program for the future of Namibia:

"To unite all Namibian people, particularly the working class, the peasantry, and progressive intellectuals into a vanguard party capable of safeguarding national independence and the building of a classless non-exploitive society based on scientific socialism ideals and principles." (6)

In general, SWAPO advocated a "national democratic revolution, to be achieved in alliance with the national bourgeoisie, as a stepping stone on the road to socialism." SWAPO promised to bring to an end "capitalist relations based on the exploitations of man." (7)

The apparent success of Soviet oriented governments coming to power in both Angola and Mozambique encouraged Nujoma to intensify his own militancy towards South Africa in Namibia. However, as indicated below, Neto's regime in Angola concluded that they could not complete their own struggle against internal opposition unless they could secure the removal of the South Africans from Namibia. Consequently, Nujoma reluctantly agreed to at least pursue negotiations with Western government and attempt to create the impression that he had an interest in peacefully resolving the conflict in Namibia.

But even while working with the various Western nations, SWAPO maintained its militant outlook concerning the future of Namibia under its rule. In an interview in Havana shortly after SWAPO agreed to negotiations with the Western nations, SWAPO's representative to the Permanent Secretariat of the Afro-Asian-Latin-American People's Solidarity Organization reviewed his organization's position. Helmut Angula asserted that SWAPO only considered the negotiations as a means of the continued struggle for liberation. He maintained SWAPO remained the only legitimate representative of the Namibian people according to the U.N. and that resolutions by the world organization would still govern any agreement.

Even though agreeing to the general framework of the Western plan for free elections leading to an independent Namibia, Nujoma indicated he had no intention of abiding to any adverse decision. In a very revealing interview with the German publication *Der Spiegel*, Nujoma dismissed the whole concept of democratic decision making.

Spiegel: Suppose the South Africans do withdraw, will you then join the Turnhalle conference?

Nujoma: The Turnhalle convention is a creature of South Africa. The SWAPO has not fought just to become part of the most fascist regime since Hitler. Do you mean to suggest we participate in it?

Spiegel: We do not want to recommend anything; we just want to know whether SWAPO is prepared to face free elections.

Nujoma: All the South Africans want to do is turn Namibia into one of their bantustans. But we are not fighting for that. We will intensify the armed struggle and kick the fascists out of Namibia, including their black puppets.

Spiegel: You mean you keep wanting war and no elections?

Nujoma: It does not make any difference, struggle or peaceful seizure of power.

Spiegel: Seizure of power by SWAPO?

Nujoma: Yes, naturally. We have fought. The power is due us. And we shall not share power with anyone.

Spiegel: This means that as far as you are concerned the

treaty of Luanda is null and void?
Nujoma: This is your interpretation.
Spiegel: Then give us your interpretation.
Nujoma: We will continue to fight, weapon in hand, until final victory. (8)

The position which Nujoma asserted in this interview in the summer of 1978 was reiterated at length again in October in Algeria in another interview, this one published in the newspaper El Moudjahid. When asked if his position had changed at all with his acceptance of the Waldheim plan for Namibian independence, Nujoma maintained that:

> SWAPO's position has not, in fact, changed at all. SWAPO demands that South Africa withdraw its illegal administration from Namibia, including Walvis Bay.... We all know that Pretoria's fascist regime is not honest or sincere in any of its negotiations. Its intentions was once again simply to use tactics to win time in which to strengthen its military position in Namibia. We have never laid down our arms. We intend to increase our efforts and liberate our country.

He went on to charge that:

> the West's intervention in Namibia is primarily aimed at saving the racist regime in Pretoria. They want to prevent us from achieving our ultimate victory. We are well aware who controls South Africa. The Western governments are now in a position to tell South Africa to accept the Security Council's report and the UN Secretary General's report. (9)

FOOTNOTES

(1) Peter Duignan and L. H. Gann, *South West Africa — Namibia*, American African Affairs Association Inc., 1978, pp. 27-28.

(2) Julian Amery, "The Crisis in Southern Africa," *Policy Review*, Fall, 1977.

(3) *FBIS*, June 13, 1978, E3.

(4) *FBIS*, August 28, 1978, E4.

(5) *FBIS*, August 10, 1978, E5.

(6) *The African Communist*, No. 68, First Quarter, 1977, p. 12, as quoted in Prinsloo, p. 18.

(7) Peter Duignan and L. H. Gann, *op. cit.*, p. 29.

(8) *FBIS*, August 1, 1978, p. E9.

(9) *FBIS*, translated from Italian, October, 1978.

CHAPTER VII

FROM THE WALDHEIM PLAN TO THE PRETORIA SUMMIT

Only four days after the return of Ambassador Ahtisaari from Namibia, Secretary General Waldheim issued his report which provided for a detailed plan for carrying out the general resolution passed by the United Nations in July. The report exacerbated already strained relations between the U.N. and South Africa as Pretoria strongly objected to many of the provisions — but indicated their willingness to study it. SWAPO did not state immediately whether they would accept the U.N. recommendations or not.

The basic provisions of the report had already been anticipated in the debate discussed above concerning the general outline accompanying the July 27th actions by the United Nations.

The overall proposal would be implemented in three stages:

1. Cessation of all hostile acts by all parties, and the withdrawal, restriction or demobilization of the various armed forces.

2. The conduct of free and fair elections to the Constituent Assembly, with pre-conditions including the repeal of restrictive laws, the release of political prisoners and voluntary return of exiles, the establishment of effective monitoring by the United Nations and an adequate period for electoral campaigning.

3. The formulation and adoption of a constitution for Namibia by the elected Assembly, to be followed by the entry into force of the constitution and the consequent achievement of the independence of Namibia.

Major controversies arose over many of the detailed proposals in the plan such as the following:

1. Elections: The report proposed that elections be delayed beyond the December 31, 1978, deadline that South Africa had previously insisted upon. The report suggested that a period of seven months should lapse "from the time the Security Council approves the plan until the elections are held." This "would allow sufficient time for the release of political prisoners, the return and registration of all Namibians outside the Territory. . . the deployment of United Nations military

and civilian personnel and electoral campaigning by all parties in an atmosphere of tranquility." Moreover, the report argued that "a majority of the political parties (in Namibia) had stressed the need for sufficient time for electoral campaigning in order to ensure free and fair balloting."

2. Size of UNTAG: The report recommended a ceiling of 9,000 men possibly being sent to Namibia to implement the overall plan for independence. This so-called United Nations Transition Assistance Group (UNTAG) would consist of 7,500 military personnel and 1,500 civilian employees.

3. U.N. Military forces: The military component would comprise infantry battalions totalling 5,000 men, plus 200 monitors along with logistic and other support elements totalling about 2,300. Thus the force size of the military had more than doubled from the initial acceptance by South Africa of Western proposals in April.

4. U.N. Civilian Force: The civilian component would consist of 1,200 persons designated to supervise and control all aspects of the electoral process and 360 civilian police officers whose duties would be to monitor the South African police in their duties to prevent intimidation or interference with the electoral process. This civilian police function had never previously arisen in either the April 25 Western plan or the U.N. proposal of July 27.

5. Costs: An initial estimate placed the cost of the entire operation at up to $300 million which would be "borne by the Member States of the United Nations." The designated size of the group and the costs involved would make the Namibia operation the largest such undertaking of the United Nations since the force sent into the Congo in 1961.

In a long letter to the Secretary General of the United Nations on September 6, 1978, R.F. Botha, the Minister of Foreign Affairs of South Africa raised severe questions about the willingness of South Africa to accept the formula for implementing the Waldheim plan. He objected to the size of the force designated for Namibia as unacceptably large, stating that:

Using the argument that under conditions of comprehensive peace there would simply be no justification for large numbers of troops, we agreed under the force of reason to an eventual reduction of our troops to 1,500. Now we find ourselves in the incredible situation where we are told that

7,500 United Nations troops would be needed to undertake tasks which under conditions of total peace we were previously assured could be administered by a few hundred.

Botha also strongly objected to the change in the timetable for elections and eventual independence for the territory, noting that:

Throughout the negotiations with the Five Western members of the Security Council, South Africa made it clear that that date must stand. This position was accepted by the Five. In fact the annexure to the proposal approved by the Security Council in Resolution 431 (1978) expressly reflects the date of independence as *"31 December 1978, at the latest."* This is clear, imperative language. The timetable was computed to attain independence by this date. This date determined the computation of the timetable and not *vice versa*. (1)

Another point raised by Botha that South Africa found unacceptable concerned the introduction of a UN civilian police force into Namibia. Referring back to the original agreement he found "no provision for a United Nations police contingent .... It does not form part of the proposal and is completely unacceptable to the South African Government." Under the original proposal sufficient latitude existed "for United Nations personnel to accompany (the existing police forces) in the performance of their duties."

Finally Botha objected to the procedures of arriving at the detailed plan without adequate consultation with South Africa. He contended that in the entire 17 day period of the visit of Ahtisaari to Namibia many of the points appearing in the Waldheim report had not even been raised in the course of discussions with Justice Steyn. In view of the explicit promise of cooperation with the Administrator General of the territory, South Africa felt the failure to consult on the basic plan could have profound adverse consequences in establishing any subsequent working arrangement with the United Nations.

Two weeks later, South African Prime Minister John Vorster simultaneously announced that he would resign his position and that his country rejected the Waldheim modifications in the plan for the independence of Namibia. He maintained that South Africa had reached complete agreement with the United

Nations on "the main elements of the dispute" which centered around the following issues: "a unitary state; universal adult suffrage; the removal of discrimination based on colour; the holding of free and fair elections; the urgency of achieving independence; the right of all South West Africans to return to participate peacefully in the political process; and the release of detainees wherever held"

What Vorster and the South Africans objected to were the four points that Foreign Minister Botha criticized on September 6th:

1. The size of the U.N. military contingent;
2. The introduction of a U.N. civil police component;
3. The lack of consultation with the Administrator General of the territory;
4. The election date.

While objecting to the modalities recommended by Waldheim for the achievement of independence for Namibia, Vorster nonetheless announced that his government would proceed with its own implementation of the original agreement of April 25th. He noted that 85 percent of the eligible voters in the territory had already registered to vote and that he would fulfill the promise to the people there of having free elections and independence by the end of the year. He announced that elections would be held in late November and welcomed international observers.

At the conclusion of these elections, Vorster left the decision to the newly elected authorities whether they wanted to "decide to draw up a constitution or postpone the drafting thereof, decide to proceed with the implementation of the proposal of the five Western nations, or decide to accept the U.N. Security Council report." (2)

Picking up the Waldheim proposal following its rejection by South Africa, the United Nations Security Council, on September 28, approved it by a 12-0 vote. Both the Soviet Union and Czechoslovakia again abstained and China did not participate. Under this resolution the United Nations

> Decided to establish, under its own authority, a United Nations Transition Assistance Group (UNTAG), in accordance with the Secretary-General's report, for a period up to 12 months, in order to assist the Secretary-General's report, for a period up to 12 months, in order to assist the

Secretary General's Special Representative for Namibia in carrying out his mandate to ensure the early independence of Namibia through free and fair elections under the supervision and control of the United Nations."

The Security Council proceeded to encourage South Africa "to co-operate with the Secretary-General in the implementation of the resolution" and declared all measures taken by South Africa relating "to the electoral process, including the unilateral registration of voters. . . null and void." The Council further requested that the Secretary General submit a new report by October 23rd on the progress of implementing the resolution.

Thus the Security Council, almost in imitation of South Africa, also decided to proceed on its own with the implementation of its plan for Namibia despite the objections of the other main party to the conflict. The United Nations ominously threatened South Africa with retaliation if she failed to cooperate. For example, the Nigerian Ambassador Lesli Harriman, declared that "South Africa has shown a death wish" and urged the Security Council to decide that "the situation constitutes a threat to international peace, and institute mandatory sanctions." Thomas Reston, speaking on behalf of the U.S. State Department contended that "The South African decision on Namibia clearly places a major obstacle in the path of an internationally acceptable settlement" and that "the question of sanctions is bound to come up" in future U.N. discussions.

But no immediate action was taken by the Security Council against South Africa. Instead intense diplomatic maneuvering transpired in the following four weeks as Western nations sought to avoid a diplomatic confrontation with South Africa. Meanwhile Pretoria indicated that the elections, initially scheduled for November, but later moved to early December, did not necessarily foreclose the possibility of later elections being conducted under U.N. auspices. In his announcement Vorster pointedly stated that his "government doesn't wish to close the doors." The U.N. made a modest effort to pacify one of South Africa's concerns by indicating that the entire UNTAG force for Namibia may not have to be as high as earlier indicated.

In a statement following the U.N. action and the often more

than subtle threats directed against his country, the new South African Prime Minister Pieter W. Botha gave the following warning:
> While we do not think we can fight the whole world, I want to give those who think they can chase us around this assurance: Don't underestimate our will to safeguard South Africa and the integrity of its borders. Don't underestimate our will to keep this an orderly community of nations. As far as Southwest Africa is concerned, don't underestimate our determination to keep peace so that the territory can find its way to self-determination in an orderly way. (3)

Meanwhile much of the discussion in the Western press proceeded to assess blame for the apparent breakdown of any mutually agreeable settlement. The leading British publication, the *Economist*, editorially charged South Africa with brushing "aside the achievements of all the long months of negotiation aimed at bringing Namibia to internationally recognized independence, and instead to push ahead with its own solution." The *Christian Science Monitor* warned that Pretoria's action "can only invite moral censure from the international community and strong action against South Africa in the form of economic sanctions. It could also lead to a widening of racial warfare in Namibia and encourgae Soviet and Cuban involvement." The *Washington Post* referred to South Africa's "rejection of the U.N. plan, which it previously accepted." The editorial contended that "it is absurd and unforgivable for South Africa to be quibbling over changes, if they are that, of such trivial dimensions, when quibbling means putting at risk the immense gains in security and respectability ensured by sticking with the U.N. plan." (4)

On the other hand, the *Wall Street Journal* noted the same concerns as the *Post* but drew opposite conclusions, stating that "it's not hard to understand South Africans' suspicions about letting such a force, [the U.N. troops] get its hands on a matter so vital to their security." The paper felt "South Africa had made major concessions" including a reduction of her own troops and admission of U.N. forces. "But by now the South Africans feel double-crossed." *To the Point* felt that the entire conflict "need not have happened. Pretoria's commitment, the West's timidity, even Waldheim's blundering arrogance could all have been overcome with more intelligent diplomacy." The magazine recalled that "The Western double-cross over Walvis Bay. . . had deeply shaken Pretoria's faith in the West's commitment to its plan for SWA. As a result Vorster agreed to proceed with it only on condition that there would be no more deviations whatever." (5) With both South Africa and black African nations in the United Nations apparently hardening their stances for a confrontation, the five Western nations instrumental in negotiating the April agreement sent their Foreign Secretaries to Pretoria. The new talks began with new threats but ended with a seemingly acceptable accommodation.

Upon his arrival in South Africa U.S. Secretary of State Vance held a 45 minute meeting with the new Prime Minister Botha. Vance delivered a personal letter from President Carter which implied that if South Africa would back down in its position on Namibia, then the United States would not bring international pressure to bear on South Africa's racial policies. Other reports indicated that the Carter Administration would offer an invitation to Botha to visit the United States.

Rather than being motivated to change basic foreign policies involving the future of a prospective neighboring state, the South African leader apparently felt affronted by such an offer. In his opening public remarks Botha told the Western foreign ministers to "Stop shouting at us. Deal with us. Stop putting stumbling blocks in our way. There is a different, wiser approach." He tried to be conciliatory by telling them "South Africa is part of the Free World and is anxious to discuss problems that have arisen between us and the rest of the family of nations." (6)

The talks progressed for three days in which South Africa succeeded in modifying the Waldheim plan once again, just as SWAPO succeeded in doing in its negotiations with first the Western powers in Luanda and then at the U.N. in New York. As the agreement re-emerged from the discussions in Pretoria, new clarifications or refinements overcame many of South Africa's basic objections. Thus the Five Western powers agreed to make a new commitment to consult with Justice Steyn concerning both the size and composition of the U.N. forces. Also they agreed to restrict the 360 man police force to simply overseeing, rather than supplanting, the existing police authorities in Namibia.

On the basic issue of elections a rather ambiguous arrangement evolved. The Western nations, with the exception of France, ominously warned South Africa either to annul the prospective elections in December or simply to assert that they consisted only of a popular opinion poll. Otherwise they indicated that they may have to consider allowing some United Nations' actions in the form of sanctions being imposed upon South Africa. The representative from France, who of the five held the lesser position of Deputy Foreign minister, apparently objected to any suggestions of sanctions as futile and counter-productive, believing that such actions would damage Western interests more than South African interests. Ultimately South Africa made only a minor concession on this issue by promising in the final communique of the meeting to use "its best efforts to persuade" the locally elected leaders of Namibia "seriously to consider ways and means of achieving international recognition through the good offices" of Ahtisaari and Steyn. Also South Africa agreed to another round of talks with U.N. representatives over Namibia.

Most of the participants hailed the meeting as successfully averting a major showdown in the U.N. Canadian Foreign Minister Donald Jamieson said the agreement with Pretoria represented "sufficient progress" to postpone any further debate or Security Council action dealing with South Africa and the Namibia question. Prime Minister Callaghan of Britain responded to the settlement as representing more progress than could have been imagined a year earlier. Meanwhile U.S. Secretary of State Vance noted that "sharp differences in views" still existed on the election issue, but that the United States would not support sanctions.

Considering the enormous pressure applied against South Africa from the time of her rejection of the Waldheim Plan, Pretoria undoubtedly exhibited tremendous diplomatic skill in her maneuvering with the Western nations. As one journal noted, South Africa "was calling the world's bluff-if it was a bluff. It seemed to be skirting the edge of disaster: diplomatic isolation, economic sanctions, escalating violence in SWA." (7) For the United States, South Africa had clearly remained a critical element of co-operation for the entire Southern Africa policy. As David Ottaway commented:

In retrospect, the fatal flaw in the administration's policy may prove to have been its awkward handling of South Africa, without whose support Washington could never have hoped to work its diplomacy in either Rhodesia or Namibia. (8)

Thus South Africa proceeded with elections prior to the end of 1978 as promised and continued to avert any severe international repercussions. In this way the timetable for complete independence with U.N. recognition would be delayed, but the likelihood of a moderate government coming to power in a neighboring territory had been enhanced. More broadly South Africa had dealt with the five major Western powers as an equal in negotiations over Namibia. She effectively ignored the U.N. Council on Namibia and managed to re-negotiate terms concerning a territory over which the United Nations claimed she had no real jurisdiction.

FOOTNOTES

(1) South African Government Press Release, emphasis in original.
(2) *Christian Science Monitor*, September 21, 1978, p. 7.
(3) *Washington Post*, October 1, 1978, p. A26.
(4) *Economist*, September 30, 1978, p. 15; *Christian Science Monitor*, September 22, 1978, p. 24; *Washington Post*, September 22, 1978, p. A16.
(5) *Wall Street Journal*, September 29, 1978; *To the Point*, September 29, 1978, p. 25.
(6) *To the Point*, October 27, 1978, p. 5, p. 9.
(7) *Ibid.*, p. 10.
(8) *Washington Post*, October 21, 1978.

CHAPTER VIII

POLITICAL PARTIES AND THE NAMIBIAN ELECTIONS

It became clear, following the meetings of Western leaders in Pretoria, that local elections would be held from December 4 to December 8 for a representative constituent assembly. The positions of all the prospective participants in such an election did not change, however, as only two significant elements of the political spectrum in Namibia agreed to participate fully in the process. The administrator of the territory, Justice Steyn, proclaimed that a substantial part of the population, 92 percent, had been duly registered and urged them to exercise their new franchise.

Major Political Parties in Namibia

For a territory with such a small population, an extraordinary range and number of political parties emerged in recent years, reflecting every ethnic, tribal, and philosophical element. In late 1977 a survey of *South West Africa/Namibia* by Gerhard Totemeyer included a very revealing table listing twenty-six identifiable political parties in Namibia as of August, 1976. Most of the parties represented single tribal or racial groups in the territory and had varying opinions on homeland policies, relations with South Africa, the United Nations and the eventual political structure desired for Namibia. This diversity has continued with the major political parties consisting of alliances between some of these innumerable small regional or ethnic parties. Only by co-operating together have many of the smaller parties been able to compete with the major Ovambo oriented parties, SWAPO, and its dissident wing, SWAPO-Democrats.

Historically, the most important parties have been SWAPO, dealt with above, and the National Party, an extension of the party of the same name in South Africa. From 1945 until 1977, the whites of the National Party dominated the limited political life of Namibia. This party regularly sent 18 members to the South African National Party conventions. Moreover, they sent six members to South Africa's House of Assembly and four senators to the upper house. Over the years 70 percent of whites, the only group with the franchise, supported the National Party candidates.

However, with the ending of the Turnhalle Conference in November, 1977, an irreconcilable split developed within the Namibian wing of the National Party. Dirk Mudge, a moderate rancher who had held the position of the party deputy leader, led a group of followers out of the party and eventually formed a broadly based coalition with the non-whites in Namibia to carry out many of the basic principles of the Turnhalle Conference. Mudge effectively drew the support of almost all representatives who had participated in the Turnhalle convention, except for a segment of whites and a few black leaders.

Thus, Mudge resigned from the National Party and formed the Republican Party from which he went on to create the Democratic Turnhalle Alliance. The DTA, as it became known, consisted of 11 different parties representing nearly all ethnic groups in Namibia, including several prominent black leaders. Among the eleven parties the most important are the South West African Peoples Democratic United Front, a Damara Party led by E.H.L. Christy; the Rehoboth Bastervereniging, an Herero Organization led by Dr. Ben Africa; the National Unity Democratic Organization, led by Chief Clemens Kapuuo until his assassination in 1978; the National Democratic Party representing an Ovambo faction of Rev. L. Ndjoba; the Labor Party, in which A.J.F. Kloppers leads a Coloured group; and the Democratic Turnhalle Party led by Nama spokesman D. Luipert. Mudge contended that only through the creation of this broadly based coalition party attempting to accommodate the tremendous diversity of Namibia could the country avoid the prospect of divisive conflict that had torn apart most other multi-ethnic African countries.

Under Mudge's effective leadership, the DTA moved away from the original Turnhalle principles by reducing the powers of the ethnic representatives and restricting their jurisdiction to their own ethnic groups and not the geographical areas that would have imitated South Africa's homelands policy. Point 2 (c) of the DTA program states: "The Alliance strives for a political system which makes it possible for the various individuals, language and population groups to maintain themselves in the cultural and material spheres and which eliminate domi-

POLITICAL PARTIES AND THE NAMIBIAN ELECTIONS   61

nation by any group." In this manner he drew the support of blacks in Namibia and separated his party from the other elements of the National Party who subsequently coalesced into AKTUR, as indicated below.

In American political terminology the DTA is usually labelled a conservative party. This derives not so much from the support for some continued recognition of ethnicity in the political structure of the country as it does from the DTA adherence to the free enterprise economic system. The DTA emphasises the value of private property in both creating agricultural incentives and productive industrial enterprises. More than other parties, except AKTUR, the DTA also advocates continued close cooperation with South Africa, particularly in economic affairs.

The DTA coupled its support from most of the moderate political elements in Namibia with significant financial backing from the business community. Critics maintained that the DTA received secret funds from South Africa but never could prove such charges. The DTA did spend far more money than any other political party on the December elections; but at the same time, it was the only nationally based party directly contesting them. In the campaign, the DTA hired 450 field workers and held regular meetings throughout the entire territory.

AKTUR or the Action Front for the Retention of Turnhalle Principles is a reactionary group firmly supporting the status quo. They support all of the original principles of the Turnhalle Constitutional Conference including, as the name implies, rigid adherences to the conclusions reached at the Turnhalle Constitutional Conferences. This includes the ethnic divisional representation of the country and, in general, allowing each ethnic group to have "the greatest possible say" in their own affairs. Thus, they believed in maintaining a limited homelands policy which would mean the continuation of exclusive ethnic zones in Namibia as well as mixed ethnical areas.

AKTUR consists of an alliance of six former political parties, most of which exclusively white and former political remnants of the National Party. But they also claimed support from some Coloureds, Basters, and the few blacks who wished to retain complete regional autonomy for their tribes. AKTUR argued that all other African countries that had attempted to institute a strict one-man one-vote mechanism of governing invariably led to the imposition of the tyrannical rule of the most powerful group over the others. Only through a limited homelands policy, similar to that advocated within South Africa itself, did AKTUR believe that Namibia could successfully navigate her way through the treacherous whirlpools of extraordinary ethnic diversity. In July 1979, the Coloured member of the AKTUR opposition party in the SWA/Namibia National Assembly, Mr. Andrew Kloppers, resigned from the party because of AKTUR's stance on the Anti-Discrimination Bill introduced into the Assembly. Mr. Kloppers then took his seat as an independent.

AKTUR information officer Ewart Benade indicated his party's reluctance to participate in the voting by stating to one reporter that "AKTUR agreed to participate in the election (only) because we had no option. It was clear that South Africa was going to hold the election and that if we refused to participate we would lose by default." The only other political organizations that agreed to participate in the December elections were three very small and ineffective parties which could only count on very narrow bases of support.

1) The Liberation Front originated in the Baster opposition party, or the Bevrydings party. Only with the coming of the December elections did it attempt to broaden its appeal and membership to other ethnic groups. Like AKTUR they supported some ethnical government division to protect rights of minorities.

2) The Herstigte Nasionale Party took a strong position to the right of AKTUR. This all-white party opposed any independence for Namibia, maintaining that only with continued South African control could the nation maintain both its security and economic viability. Thus it supported the implementation of an apartheid system as developed in the Odendaal Plan of the 1960s.

3) The Namibian Christian Democratic Party only came into existence in late October, 1978, for the express purpose of posing another alternative to the AKTUR and the DTA. This party ironically opposed the right of the Constituent Assembly elected in December from exercising any authority. They maintained that only an election under U.N. auspices should be recognized as a valid mechanism for attaining independence. This position

of the party provided a clear opportunity for groups dissenting to the election process to express themselves.

Dissenting Democratic Groups

Opposition to the elections included many of the most important groups that eventually would have to be accommodated in the political structure of the territory. The Namibian National Front (NNF) called on the people of Namibia "not to legitimize a neo-colonial, reactionary and illegal process" by participating in the December elections.

The Namibia National Front consists of an alliance of six white and black political parties. These included the South West African National Union, led by Gerson Veii; the National Independence Party of Charly Hartung; the Federal Party, chaired by Brian O'Lynn; the Darmara Tribal Council led by Justus Garoeb; and the Mbanderu tribe. Thus the NNF represents a loose coalition of various ethnic groups concentrated in most of the non-Ovambo sections of Namibia and hence presumably possesses a broad appeal as a major party.

The NNF strongly opposes South African rule over Namibia, but at the same time also opposes SWAPO. They favor progressive evolutionary change in the direction of a liberal social democracy. They reject both ethnicity and regionalism in favor of individualism; but nonetheless also support a unicameral parliament with strong centralized governmental powers. While at some times favoring free enterprise, they also support some nationalization and socialist redistribution of the wealth of the territory. Possibly the group too closely resembles a European socialist party in orientation and thus has never realized its potential popular appeal in the Namibian context of politics.

During the December elections, the NNF requested "South Africa to scrap its new devices and to render the necessary cooperation to the contact group of the five Western powers that will result in an internationally recognized solution." Believing that another election would take place later, NNF Information Secretary Reinhard Rukoro noted that: "We have decided to ignore the whole election as a non-event and concentrate our efforts on the second election under U.N. supervision."

SWAPO-Democrats similarly took the position that the elections were meaningless: "We are not calling for a boycott," asserted Party President Andreas Shipanga. "People must be free to vote or not to vote. To advocate a boycott would be a tactical error."

As noted above, SWAPO-Democrats came into being as various dissident members of Nujoma's organization returned to Namibia and attempted to establish an alternative political force to appeal to the large Ovambo population in the territory. They hoped to draw substantial support from their former SWAPO colleagues and among their fellow Ovambos. While generally supporting the social policies of SWAPO they nonetheless rejected both the anti-democratic elements in Nujoma's philosophy and his close association with Marxism.

SWAPO-Democrats entered into a close alliance with the NNF and challenged the December elections together. The rhetoric of both groups remained sharply critical of both South Africa and SWAPO. A week before the election, one of the executive members of SWAPO-Democrats, Dr. Kenneth Abrahams, announced that his party had just drafted a new constitution. Under this constitution, he emphasized that "We fully support the policy manifesto of the Namibia National Front and we have pledged ourselves to work with the NNF for the unification of all democratic forces in Namibia today." Sounding like SWAPO, he noted that South Africa's grant of independence to the territory did not mean an end to the liberation struggle but only that it had entered a new phase that could only be consummated with internationally supervised elections.(1)

SWAPO

SWAPO firmly opposed the elections and continued to insist that they would win any fair election. According to SWAPO Treasurer Lucas Pohamba, they represented "the aspirations of the Namibian people." He threatened South Africa to "come to their senses" and either accept the Waldheim plan or be driven from Namibia "like the Americans from Vietnam." (2)

SWAPO expressed skepticism that any U.N. supervised election would follow the December elections. A statement issued by their organization in Windhoek noted that "South Africa has not given any guarantees concerning the holding of a second election in the territory next year under the supervision of the United Nations." Thus they predicted that the December elections would only serve as "a face-saving device" for South

Africa "withdrawing from the whole settlement plan by giving the impression that it is now an issue between the United Nations and the so-called elected people of Namibia."

As the election campaign progressed, SWAPO denounced the political activities with increasing stridency. One commentary referred to any decisions rendered as "null and void" and that "made our position vividly clear, that independence of Namibia will only come through the barrel of the gun." The precise tactics of SWAPO opposition became confusing, however, as different and sometimes contradictory instructions flowed from various SWAPO sources. On November 1, 1978, the Voice of Namibia. broadcasting from Luanda, Angola, proclaimed that "the Namibian workers are not going to take part in nonsensical elections" and that SWAPO "will give orders that all the Namibian workers should abandon mines and other industrial establishments" as a protest on election day. (3)

However, a week later, Mokganedi Tghabanello, SWAPO Publicity and Information Secretary, repudiated any SWAPO support for a strike during the December elections, stating that "We are definitely not busy organizing a strike." At the same time, he did call on all SWAPO supporters to boycott the elections. Confusion continued as reports appeared that Jomo Outjou, SWAPO's secretary of labor, had called for placards being drawn up to announce a strike. Havana radio broadcast that SWAPO called for an 8-day general strike beginning on December 1, 1978, to protest the election going on in Namibia. This finally led to SWAPO's top official in Namibia, Daniel Tjongarero, to once again state that "It is not our intention to hold a strike, not even as far as our colleagues outside the country are concerned." But he reiterated the call for a boycott in order to inform SWAPO supporters "what the election means; that the government is seeking a mandate through the December election to reject any cooperation with the international community in trying for a peaceful solution."

Several days prior to the opening of elections, Sam Nujoma announced that SWAPO would attempt through violence to prevent them. In an interview with the Milan newspaper *Il Giornale* during a Rome meeting of the Conference on Solidarity, Nujoma asserted that "the December elections in Namibia will be invalid and illegal. We have asked the Namibian population to boycott the elections and we will even try to prevent them from taking place by stepping up the armed struggle." Reiterating his previous views of democratic processes, he said "The elections do not interest us and we cannot accept any mediation from Western nations which we consider our enemies." (4)

The disinterest of SWAPO in the electoral processes remains one of the most enigmatic aspects of the Namibian problem to many Western observers. Many commentators on Namibia, weighing the population strength of the Ovambo, have predicted that SWAPO would either win clear majority in any election or at least be the most powerful party in the territory. In either case elections would presumably offer SWAPO a better chance to come to power than any political group in Namibia. But, as the quote from Nujoma above indicates, SWAPO has little interest or use in elections. One of the leading experts on Namibian politics, G.K.H. Totemeyer, has provided an excellent summary of the reasons for SWAPO's reluctance to enter elections.

> The Swapo leadership is not altogether sure whether more than fifty percent of the voters will actually vote for Swapo in an election. Secondly, Swapo would like to take over the political regime in Namibia as the undisputed and sole representative political organization as did Machel in Mozambique and Neto in Angola. Thirdly, if Swapo would be prepared to take part in a democratically fought election as one among many other political parties and groupings, this could harm its image and claim of being the only and authentic political representative of the Namibian people. Swapo is recognized as such by the UNO and the OAU. In other words, for Swapo its participation in a free and democratic election could mean a loss of face and stature in international politics, while at the same time it runs the risk of not being voted in as the governing party. (5)

The Election Campaign

During the campaign the DTA pressed as hard for a large turnout as they did for their own platform for support. They realized, as did AKTUR and the other parties, that a large number of voters would undoubtedly benefit the better known DTA party, particularly since it had a much broader appeal than the other parties. Also, the DTA acknowledged that they tacitly ran against the combined campaigns of SWAPO, SWAPO-D and the NNF who all urged boycotts or non-participation in the elections. The DTA campaigned vigorously as the party which had most effectively promoted the independence of Namibia and therefore deserved credit in the form of votes for the freedom they had apparently won from South Africa.

With AKTUR as the only meaningful, yet weak, opposition on the ballot, the campaign turned often rankerous between various elements òf the white population. Particularly vitriolic exchanges took place between the Nationalist newspaper *Die Suidwester* and *Republikein* of the Republican Party (part of the DTA). The main issue between them consisted of their conflicting attitudes towards the Turnhalle Convention and the role of ethnicity in the division and government of the country. AKTUR maintained support for original Turnhalle principles, while Mudge and some of his followers promised a substantial alteration of these principles by abandoning the rigid ethnic divisions. AKTUR maintained that failure to recognize distinct tribal divisions would ultimately lead to dissolution of the country into civil war, while the DTA argued that the differences between the various tribes could be accommodated within a democratic framework. Both parties argued that only their platforms could effectively stave off the threat of SWAPO to Namibia.

The DTA conducted an enormous and expensive campaign complete with bumper stickers, meetings featuring free food and beer, and mass rallies of people throughout the country. On election day, they drew attention to the voting and their own party by erecting huge campaign tents often dwarfing in size the nearby polling stations themselves.

As the DTA attempted to campaign in all sections of Namibia, they ran into particular harassment in the northern part of the country, the stronghold of SWAPO. Various guerrilla attacks during the campaign led black supporters of the DTA to arm themselves when campaigning in Ovamboland. DTA leader Dirk Mudge defended the action by arguing that "Every white man in this country has got a gun or rifle, but these black people have nothing and they are living on the border with Angola." He charged that members of SWAPO were coming over the border to kill black DTA supporters "so we are going to help these people to defend themselves." Nonetheless, the DTA campaigned with particular intensity in Ovamboland and other territories comprising the northern borderland of Namibia.

South Africa charged that SWAPO had been attempting to subvert the elections. The commander of the South African forces in the northern area of Namibia (Number Two Military Area), claimed that SWAPO forces had been both spreading rumors that the elections had been postponed and also threatening revenge against anyone participating in the polling. He charged that 18 people in the Ovambo area had been murdered by SWAPO in recent months, most of them DTA organizers. More broadly he announced that during the previous six months 75 skirmishes with SWAPO terrorists had taken place as well as 83 landmines incidents, 16 acts of sabotage, and 26 abductions.

During the campaign, AKTUR attempted to implicate the DTA in the Government Information Office scandal in South Africa. The Vice Chairman of AKTUR, Percy Niehaus, demanded to know whether any of the South African secret funds involved in an Information Office scandal had been used for political purposes in Namibia. AKTUR estimated that total expenditure in the campaign would be around $350,000 which is what they charged the DTA with spending during each month of the previous year.

In order to encourage the participation of SWAPO, Justice Steyn released 26 members of that organization from detention. As SWAPO and other parties indicated that they would boycott the elections, Steyn nonetheless encouraged them to participate in public discussion and debate so that they could fully express to the people their reasons for urging non-participation.

SWAPO and other groups opposed to the elections being held without U.N. control took up Steyn's offer and took part in many public gatherings during the course of the campaign and urged the people of the territory not to participate in the December voting.

The tacit participation of SWAPO in the electoral process even while campaigning against voting reflected the broader irony of the political situation in Namibia. As *New York Times* columnist Tom Wicker wrote from Windhoek:

> One of Namibia's oddities is that although SWAPO carries on guerrilla warfare against South African troops in

the north near the Angolan border, the party has public offices right across Kaiserstrasse from the post office in Windhoek. (6)

Allowing the continued existence of an internal operating wing of SWAPO in Namibia indicated a greater willingness of South Africa to tolerate dissent in the midst of war than nearly any other African governments have allowed even in peace a decade after independence.

FOOTNOTES

(1) *FBIS*, November 28, 1978, p. E3, Pretoria broadcast.
(2) *FBIS*, October 25, 1978, p. E6.
(3) *FBIS*, November 2, 1978, p. E3; *FBIS*, November 3, 1978, p. E2.
(4) Rome ANSA broadcast, from *FBIS*, November 29, 1978, p. E4.
(5) G. K. H. Totemeyer, "Political Groupings in Namibia — Their Role and Chances," *International Affairs Bulletin*, Vol. 2, No. 1, 1978, p. 29.
(6) Tom Wicker, "Confusion in Africa," *New York Times*, December 3, 1978, p. E19.

CHAPTER IX

SOUTH AFRICA, THE U.N. AND ELECTIONS

Following the meeting of the five foreign ministers with South African leaders in October, the United Nations again took up the issue of Namibia in early November. They had delayed further consideration of the Waldheim Plan until additional negotiations had been completed. Although South Africa agreed to continue negotiations, African delegates at the U.N. nonetheless called for a full-scale economic embargo against South Africa both for allegedly failing to proceed swiftly with implementation of the Waldheim Plan and also for allowing elections to take place in early December. A draft resolution by the Africans proposed that sanctions be imposed if South Africa did not cancel the proposed elections within two weeks.

In the General Assembly debate, the five Western nations opposed any use of a complete embargo or even the threat of one at this time. They asserted that the elections in December should be regarded as "null and void," but that South African willingness to hold subsequent U.N. supervised elections should be the standard used for considering taking drastic actions against South Africa. A milder resolution drafted by India and supported by several African countries, including Nigeria and Gabon, eventually passed. This set a deadline of November 25 for the Secretary-General to submit another report to the General Assembly indicating whether South Africa would cooperate with the U.N. plan for Namibia. The resolution threatened that if South Africa declined the U.N. should "meet forthwith to initiate appropriate actions under the charter, including Chapter VII thereof," i.e., the enforcement section dealing with sanctions. This resolution passed by a 10-0 vote, but all five Western members of the Security Council abstained. With nine affirmative votes necessary for passage, the resolution just narrowly succeeded.

In a speech to the Foreign Policy Association at the time of the U.N. vote, Ambassador Andrew Young suggested that some sanctions might be used against South Africa to secure her cooperation. Reportedly under consideration were a ban on air travel between South Africa and Western nations and limited economic sanctions on credits and loans to South Africa.

On November 25, 1978, South African Foreign Minister Pik Botha travelled to New York to meet with Kurt Waldheim to continue discussions of implementing the U.N. plan for independence for Namibia. Among the issues discussed included the number of U.N. troops stationed in Namibia during the transition period to independence, their countries of origin and the precise role and purpose of the U.N. police force personnel. President Carter also met with Botha at this time and warned him of "real problems" if South Africa failed to cooperate with the United Nations in Namibia.

In an interview in Britain, Botha warned the Western nations that "there is a point beyond which we will not be pushed" on the U.N. plan for Namibia. "We want international recognition for the territories, sure, but not a second Angola or Rhodesia situation." Therefore he renewed a major objection to the U.N. plan by stating that "We cannot accept thousands and thousands of U.N. troops which would in effect make a fair election impossible."

To threats of U.N. sanctions and other attacks against South Africa he said: "It astonishes me that Western governments and other circles in the U.N. can continue talking about South Africa being in the wrong. What must happen is SWAPO must be told they must make a choice between terrorism and elections. It is not South Africa that is delaying anything."

Although willing to later advise the leaders elected in early December to work with the U.N., South Africa nonetheless maintained that the elections themselves remained an authentic political process for the creation of an independent Namibia. South African Foreign Minister Pik Botha asserted that "This election is taking place in terms of the Western proposals accepted in April by South Africa and all the parties participating in this election." In the midst of the campaign Steyn reiterated this view that whoever won the December election would have to decide about independence and whether another election should be held in 1979. (1)

Media and Elections

In order to bolster international support for the December elections, the territorial administrator issued invitations to come to Namibia to about one hundred foreign newsmen, including members of the United Nations press corps. The expenses of those invited would be born by his administration and the newsmen were encouraged to arrive several days prior to the elections and remain until they concluded. He hoped that their reporting would indicate that a genuinely democratic process had taken place and that charges of fraud and coercion could be effectively refuted.

The invitations arose in the wake of the failure of official observers coming for the elections. As Steyn said, "I have repeatedly asked the U.N. and the five Western powers to send observers to monitor the election, but they have not made use of my offer." (2)

Meanwhile, SWAPO attempted to dissuade any journalists from overseeing the election process. A SWAPO official in Dar es Salaam informed any journalists going to Namibia that they would be subsequently blacklisted. A voice of Namibia broadcast from Tanzania warned "the capitalist foreign journalists" coming for the elections that "We will consider such people as an enemy of the Namibia revolution and they will not escape the consequences of such an obvious form of collaboration with the racist regime of South Africa." (3) This led to the South-West African police chief to denounce the SWAPO threats and announce that the safety of foreign newsmen could be guaranteed by his forces.

The United Nations Council on Namibia joined in the dispute by charging that the invitation to foreign journalists was only a bogus public relations stunt by South Africa to imply that fair elections took place. Justice Steyn responded that only reputable journalists had been invited and that he only sought to have the truth emerge concerning the December elections.

Bombings

Isolated threats of violence erupted in a series of dramatic bombings in downtown Windhoek just two days prior to the opening of elections. A series of three explosions, the first acts of urban terrorism in Namibia, took place with one in a large department store wounding 14 shoppers. The police quickly ordered all stores in the area closed. Earlier that same day about 50 SWAPO supporters had held a march in the downtown area to protest the forthcoming elections. This had led to sporadic mob violence. Following the explosions police arrested five leaders of SWAPO in Windhoek and detained many of the demonstrators. Just prior to his arrest, SWAPO spokesman Mogkanedi Tlhabanello denied responsibility for the bombings and instead charged that they were part of an "anti-SWAPO campaign." Another SWAPO spokesman, Jason Angula assumed "that the bombs were installed by AKTUR or the South African police." However, Sam Nujoma later said that "On Saturday (the day of the bombing), in Windhoek, our people continued to resist." Administrator Steyn thus blamed SWAPO for the explosions. (4)

Elections

Despite the ominous violence during the campaign and bombings in Windhoek, the elections proceeded from December 4 to 8 with only minor difficulties. SWAPO demonstrators arrested following the bombings were released the day elections began, although the six leaders remained in custody. Only two small clashes took place between South African security forces and SWAPO, one near a polling place in Ovambo. Police detained eight members of the NNF charging them with trying to seize registration cards from voters. Voting progressed for four days in a nearly festive atmosphere. While military and police forces remained on alert, they were not conspicuous around polling places. During the voting, an especial effort was made in northern Namibia, where most terrorist incidents had taken place in recent months, to bring out the vote. This involved using 120 fixed and nine mobile polling booths in the area and succeeded in drawing out most of the Ovambos despite threats from SWAPO that polling places in the area were being watched and reprisals would be taken against participants.

With diverse polling places, cumbersome paper ballots, and inexperience in dealing with elections, the final results of the balloting did not become available until December 15. At that time the DTA was declared the overwhelming winner, receiving 268, 130 votes out of a total cast òf 326, 264, for 82.1 percent. AKTUR finished a very poor second with only 38,716 votes. Perhaps most significant was the relatively small abstention vote of 81,580 or less than 20 percent of all registered voters. As indicated on the chart below the domination of the

DTA in the balloting stretched across every possible evaluation of the vote as they received a total vote of over 60 percent of the entire Namibian population eligible to vote. The complete vote breakdown and allocation of representatives in the Constituent Assembly were as follows:

December Election Vote

Party or Category	Total Vote	Percentage Party Vote	Percentage All Votes	Percentage Eligible Votes	Assembly Seats
Democratic Turnhalle Alliance	268,130	82.1	65.0	60.5	41
Action Front for the Preservation of the Turnhalle Principles	38,716	11.9	9.4	8.7	6
Namibia Christian Democratic Party	9,073	2.8	2.2	2.0	1
The Herstigte Nastionale Partey	5,781	1.8	1.4	1.3	1
The Liberation Front	4,564	1.4	1.1	1.1	1
Spoiled ballots	4,791	—	1.1	1.1	—
Abstentions	81,580	—	19.8	18.4	—
Non-registered	30,806	—	—	6.9	—

Source: Bulletin No. 1, 1979, Africa Institute of South Africa.

With 441,000 registered voters, the 326,264 votes cast represented 80.3 percent of the total electorate. Such a large turnout indicated a substantial repudiation of SWAPO, the NNF and SWAPO-democrats who all advised people not to vote in the elections. It clearly demonstrated that the aggressive campaign by SWAPO to discourage voter participation had failed miserably.

As the *Economist* stated following the election: "The fact that so many people braved SWAPO's threats suggests that its influence is not as strong as that exercised by local chiefs in tribal areas and by employers in the towns." (5)

Prior to the election most observers felt that a turnout of over 50 percent would indicate a repudiation of SWAPO by the voters and the size of vote beyond that amount would reveal the organizational ability of the DTA to marshall support.

Demonstrating this ability to generate support, even against only very weak opposition, could prove very useful in a subsequent election in which the people will have already learned how to vote for the DTA.

The breadth of the DTA victory also eradicated much of the concern that the election would lead to racial polarization in Namibia with most of the whites voting for the AKTUR. The leader of AKTUR warned that "The majority of the whites will not accept Mudge as their leader." However the results indicated that, once again confounding forecasters, a majority of the white vote went to the DTA and not to AKTUR and the other smaller parties. Thus a moderate consensus appeared to emerge among both the whites, blacks and coloreds in Namibia as they all supported the DTA.

SWAPO, however, charged that massive fraud characterized the voting. Nujoma claimed that his own sources in Namibia indicated that the results did not reflect real attitudes of Namibians because one-third of the voters were white residents of Namibia, soldiers and policemen, one-sixth belonged to UNITA and FNLA groups from Angola, one-third were workers and old people forced to vote, and one-eighth consisted of votes cast for dead people. This curious arithmetic left only one-twenty-fourth (1/24) of the vote for everyone else. Another SWAPO spokesman, Philip Djerije (acting publicity secretary) asserted that 100,000 black workers were "virtually subjected" to the will of their employers during the election. Moreover, he estimated the total population of the territory at 1.2 million and thus the percent turnout at the polls actually was much lower than it appeared.

The rationalization of SWAPO failed to conceal the magnitude of their defeat. The figures in the voting were simply too conspicuous to ignore. Even in the SWAPO stronghold of Ovamboland in the north, 116,000 people voted, or 35.6 percent of the entire vote cast in Namibia. This boded especially badly for any future election in which the basic strength of SWAPO had to emerge from this particular tribal area. Moreover, the inability to intimidate voters into boycotting the elections in this area near the Angolan border revealed how ineffective their strategy had been.

The change in a six year period had been dramatic. In 1973, SWAPO also called upon the people in Ovamboland to boycott elections to the Legislative Council and then only 2.5 percent of the electorate went to the polls. (6)

While everyone expected a DTA victory at the polls in December, few commentators expected either the magnitude of that victory or the extraordinarily large turnout of registered voters. The surprising results ultimately led to confidence in the DTA that they could triumph in later internationally supervised elections and led South Africa to conclude that a substantial moderate majority existed in the population of Namibia.

The U.N. and the December Elections

Following the elections in December, the United Nations' General Assembly took up the Namibia issue. This time, following a debate that reiterated most of the same points raised earlier, the U.N. unanimously passed two resolutions condemning South Africa and urging Security Council action. The first resolution, passed 120-0 with 19 abstentions, urged the Security Council "to take effective measures, including sanctions . . . particularly the imposition of comprehensive economic sanctions, including a trade embargo, an oil embargo, and a complete arms embargo." A second resolution, passed 123-0 with 16 abstentions, charged that the failure of South Africa to comply with previous U.N. resolutions and the Waldheim Plan constituted a threat to international peace and security and thus punishable under the U.N. Charter.

The threat to peace, as in Rhodesia against whom sanctions presently apply, presumably consisted of guerrilla warfare being launched to change the status quo. Once again, the U.N. allowed a very liberal interpretation of Article VII to override the clear language of Article III which prohibits interference in the internal affairs of other countries. On both of the resolutions, the United States abstained along with other Western powers, but on the grounds that a settlement could be reached and not that such actions were necessarily inappropriate eventually.

Election Aftermath

Upon completion of the elections, a new Constituent Assembly promptly met on December 20, 1978, in Windhoek at the Turnhalle Convention Hall. The new Assembly represented all segments of the population as the DTA distributed its 41 seats among the various tribal groups. They nominated four representatives each for the Ovambos, the Hereros, the Kavangos, the Caprivians, the whites, the Namas, the coloreds and the Damaras, as well as three representatives each for the Basters, the bushmen and the Tswana. Meanwhile, AKTUR, alloted six seats, distributed them to four whites, one colored and one Baster. The three other parties each had only one seat which they alloted to their leaders. Justice Steyn urged the Assembly to consider a second election under U.N. supervision as the top priority. He noted that "It is a miracle that the election of this assembly was completed in such a peaceful, efficient and convincing manner, and in spite of continued efforts on a wide front to disrupt and even destroy it." (7)

Both South African Prime Minister P. W. Botha and its Foreign Minister Pik Botha traveled to Windhoek to persuade the Assembly to take part in the U.N. supervised elections. At a news conference upon his arrival Pieter Botha stated "We are prepared to have another election here. We have advised the elected representatives that they should accept it." At the same time they sent two letters to Waldheim indicating both objections and cooperation with the implementation of U.N. plans for Namibia. While promising to work with the U.N. in implementing Security Council Resolution 435, they also objected to continued recognition and support for SWAPO in the U.N. Moreover, they emphasized the need to monitor SWAPO military bases and secure the release of political detainees held by SWAPO. Finally, South Africa reaffirmed its intention not to withdraw any of its estimated 25,000 troops stationed in Namibia until violence in the territory had ceased.

Dirk Mudge, Chairman of the DTA quickly set two conditions for further negotiations with the United Nations on another election: 1) that such elections be held quickly and 2) that nothing in the procedures would work to the disadvantage of moderate parties such as the DTA.

At a press conference Mudge told reporters "We do not know whether or not there will be a second election." He repeated early South African concerns that the U.N., with its support for SWAPO, could make a future election unfair. A U.N. supervised election would provide a "built-in" advantage for SWAPO or other political parties because, according to the U.N., SWAPO is the "sole authentic representative of the people of Namibia." Therefore, Mudge argued "if the U.N. will eliminate this and other objections, we will be prepared to talk and state our point of view." (8) Mudge proposed that any new elections be held prior to August 31, 1979, and that the U.N. withdraw its recognition and support for SWAPO and proclaim neutrality in the elections.

Despite objections raised by the other parties, the DTA dominated Assembly approved a resolution accepting United Nations supervised election in the territory in the next year. The Assembly requested that the U.N. Security Council respond by January 28, 1979 to its proposal.

As the Assembly met, the authorities moved towards reconciliation with SWAPO by releasing its six leaders who had been arrested at the time of the bombings. After being held under the Terrorist Act, no charges were filed against the six. SWAPO's secretary for information and publicity in Zambia, Peter Katjavivi, quickly issued a statement from Zambia that they would be willing to proceed with implementation of the U.N. plan. At the same time other SWAPO representatives threatened to intensify the armed struggle in Namibia if South Africa failed to accept the U.N. plan.

In order to partly accommodate one of the concerns of the DTA, Kurt Waldheim announced that the U.N. would no longer recognize SWAPO as the only representative of the people of Namibia. This led representatives of the DTA and the NNF to both commend his statement, but also urged the General Assembly to formally approve such a change of policy for it to become effective.

Upon receiving results of the election the NNF called again for new elections and urged cooperation with the U.N. The large turnout only represented a yearning for independence according to the NNF which reaffirmed that "Without the participation of the United Nations, a credible registration process, and independent press. . . there cannot be a free and fair election campaign." (9)

More broadly the NNF contended that Namibia would ultimately face disaster if the DTA attempted to run the country. John S. Kirkpatrick, Treasurer of the NNF predicted that any DTA government would only lead to the imposition of sanctions against South Africa and Namibia. "The guerrilla war will be intensified, and with heavy Communist support. SWAPO will declared itself the government-in-exile. There's a very grave danger of foreign power, such as Cuba or East Germany, intervening to support SWAPO." (10) Thus the Namibian National Front supported further negotiations between South Africa and the U.N. leading to new elections. NNF Publicity Secretary Reinhardt Rukoro said that they would be willing to participate in "free, fair and democratic" elections. "But the kind of elections in which we agree to take part must only be for the independence of Namibia and not for an advisory body or council." (11)

While the NNF and other parties all continued to participate in the political processes in Namibia, the DTA clearly had the upper hand among the various internal parties in the wake of their victory. They could even effectively challenge the external wing of SWAPO in any upcoming political battle for control of the territory. Through an active role in the administration of the territory over the next nine months, the DTA could consolidate political power won in the December voting. Using its dominating strength in the Constituent Assembly the DTA could act with the territorial administration while other political groups could only continue to talk. The image of power may be particularly important to the people of the territory who have usually functioned politically within tribal and other structures with considerable respect endangered for designated authorities. This advantage can be enhanced if the DTA pledge to work for full removal of discriminatory practices in the territory can be fulfilled. One of the earliest motions coming before the Constituent Assembly dealt with the elimination of all remaining discriminatory practices.

Thus, as *To the Point* commented, the "DTA control of the assembly will give the moderate alliance a freer hand to introduce reforms which would both undercut the support of SWAPO and persuade elements of other political groupings ... to join forces with it." (12)

The DTA legal advisor, Fanuel Kozonguizi expressed the same view by pointing out that "While negotiating over the second election, the Constituent Assembly will be able to introduce changes that are of importance to the ordinary people."

Thus the real question concerning the future of political

developments in Namibia shifted once again to the U.N. and the maneuvering by SWAPO to gain through negotiations what they had lost through December elections. Vitally important psychological momentum favored the DTA following the elections and SWAPO became fearful that unless the course of events were substantially altered they could not come to power in Namibia even in U.N. supervised elections.

FOOTNOTES

(1) *FBIS*, November 14, 1978, E7.
(2) *FBIS*, November 8, 1978, E4.
(3) *FBIS*, December 3, 1976, E6.
(4) *FBIS*, December 4, 1978, E5; *FBIS*, December 7, 1978, E5.
(5) "First Things Should Come First," *The Economist*, December 16, 1978, p. 51.
(6) "Decolonization: Issue on Namibia," U.N., December, 1977.
(7) *FBIS*, December 21, 1978, E2.
(8) *FBIS*, December 22, 1978, E4.
(9) *FBIS*, December 13, 1978, E4.
(10) Richard R. Leger, "Namibia Is Due to Become World's Newest Nation Next Month — and Probably Its Newest Hot Spot," *Wall Street Journal*, November 21, 1978, p. 78.
(11) *FBIS*, January 5, 1979, E2.
(12) *To the Point*, December, 1978, p. 32.

CHAPTER X
SOUTH AFRICA, THE U.N. AND ELECTIONS

As the new year opened the prospects for a negotiated settlement in Namibia again seemed quite possible. The South African leaders meetings with the newly elected leaders in Windhoek in late December had led to a new agreement "to cooperate in the expeditious implementation of Security Council Resolution 435 (1978)." (footnote letter from Minister of Foreign Affairs of South Africa to the U.N. Secretary General.) In the formal letter of agreement indicating this willingness to proceed, the South African Foreign Minister also raised five specific points related to the negotiated settlement: South African troop strength would only be reduced upon "a comprehensive cessation of violence and hostilities," elections would "take place not later than 30 September, 1979," SWAPO bases in neighboring states must be monitored as provided in paragraph 12 of the April 1978 agreement, law and order would remain "the primary responsibility of the existing police forces," and the Administrator-General would exercise legislative and administrative authority "during the transitional period until independence."

In his response to this letter, Secretary-General Waldheim acknowledged the five points raised by R. F. Botha, specifically agreeing with the need for a comprehensive peace and the 30 September, 1979 deadline. Also he agreed with the need for monitoring SWAPO bases by noting that "Certainly paragraph 12 of the settlement proposal is a very important element, and I have been assured by representatives of the States which border on Namibia that they will co-operate fully with the United Nations in ensuring that UNTAG is able to carry out its mandate." (footnote: Letter of 1 January from Secretary-General Waldheim to the Minister of Foreign Affairs R. F. Botha of South Africa).

In order to work out the final details of the settlement, Waldheim sent a new mission to Namibia on January 13, 1979, once again headed by Ambassador Ahtisaari. Accompanied by 20 advisors, he consulted with Justice Steyn in order to proceed with the implementation of the U.N. Resolution 435 for new elections in Namibia. He indicated a willingness to accomodate many of the concerns expressed by South Africa and the newly elected Constituent Assembly. He stated, e.g., that registration of voters would be organized by the Administrator General under the supervision of the United Nations and thus there might be no need for completely new registration of voters.

In later meetings in Cape Town with Roelof Botha, Ahtisaari pledged that the UNTAG would be completely impartial in its dealings with all political parties in the territory. He maintained that previous U.N. support for SWAPO had consisted of particular programs of assistance and did not indicate political support for the organization. Also he promised close supervision of the return of exiles to Namibia in order to guarantee that only people originally from the territory could re-enter to participate in the elections.

The DTA expressed satisfaction with the discussions with Ahtisaari and emphasized the importance of a cease fire preceeding any withdrawal of South African troops. As he left South Africa, Ahtisaari indicated that the neighboring countries of Angola, Zambia and Botswana would all cooperate with the United Nations in Namibia. He suggested that SWAPO bases in these areas would be monitored by U.N. forces during the transition period to elections. In Namibia itself he expected 24 United Nations working centers being established to carry out the now modified Waldheim Plan.

Military representatives from the U.N. and South Africa also met and reached a basic agreement on the implementation of the security aspects of the U.N. Resolution. They drafted a very detailed nine stage plan for the deployment of UNTAG forces and the relative positions and responsibilities of the forces of South Africa and SWAPO. The entire process begins with "A cessation of all hostile acts by all parties . . . . "

Unfortunately, new complications quickly developed with the series of meetings held by Ahtisaari in the Front Line states. Issues seemingly resolved in meetings in Namibia and South Africa rapidly appeared to unravel. One of the first conflicts to arise concerned the release of prisoners prior to any election in Namibia. In his meetings with front line states. Ahtisaari quickly accepted the position of those countries, particularly Zambia, that they did not have any SWAPO dissidents imprisoned in their territories. Ahtisaari thus informed both the authorities in Namibia and South Africa they should quit pressing this issue and that he would give the question no further attention until they provided him with a list of names and locations of the alleged detentions.

This position of Ahtisaari drew sharp reactions from both South Africa and SWAPO-Democrats. South Africa pointed out that the five Western powers had acknowledged the existence of the camps in Zambia and Tanzania at the time of their discussion with Pretoria in June, 1977. Moreover additional information, including a comprehensive list of names, had been given to Ahtisaari in August, 1978. Botha contended that the skepticism concerning the detentions "displays so much ignorance or partiality to SWAPO that I can barely believe that a man in his position could have said it." (1)

The position of Ahtisaari also came under sharp attack by SWAPO Democrats, some of whose leaders had only been released from such camps the previous year. Dr. Kenneth Abrahams issued the following statement in Windhoek:

We in the SWAPO Democrats have been very surprised at the latest utterances made by Mr. Martti Ahtisaari in which he says that people should stop allegations about the existence of concentration camps in Zambia. Now Mr. Martti Ahtisaari has been the UN high commissioner for Namibia since 1976 and these people who are detained in Zambia have been in these concentration camps since April 1976. In other words, we're speaking of a period of about 3 years. Now, in this time we have informed the United Nations Council for Namibia and we have informed Mr. Ahtisaari in his capacity as UN commissioner for Namibia about these camps and about these 200 Namibians who have been detained in Zambia because of their opposition to the SWAPO president, Sam Nujoma. Now, in addition to the numerous petitions which we have sent to Mr. Ahtisaari, we have also sent him a list of names, a list containing the names of some of the people detained in these camps and we have also given him a list of these camps themselves. (2)

At the same time Andreas Shipanga challenged the Zambian government to allow him into their country to point out the precise locations of the camps which he maintained still held an estimated 1,800 prisoners. He accused Zambian government officials of lying to United Nations authorities who then naively accepted the lies despite lists of names and locations previously provided them.

Neither Zambia nor any of the other Front Line states acknowledged the imprisonment of SWAPO dissidents and adamantly refused to allow any impartial observer force to investigate the charges made by South Africa and SWAPO dissidents. This dispute would continue, however, other more significant conflicts quickly overshadowed concerns about the fate of the SWAPO dissidents.

The meetings in Angola with President Neto and SWAPO leader Nujoma raised new fundamental issues in the settlement proposal dealing with the question of a cease-fire, the monitoring of military bases, and a prospective armed SWAPO force gathering at bases within Namibia. Nujoma raised these new issues following his meeting with Ahtisaari by charging South Africa with "putting forth new pre-conditions regarding the implementation of the United Nations plan for Namibia's independence." He specifically rejected "the idea that SWAPO guerrilla forces will be confined to bases outside Namibia in the neighboring countries and be monitored there." He also denounced any "reception centers" inside Namibia as "concentration camps" and demanded that South African troops would have to withdraw beginning on the date of the cease-fire and deployment of UNTAG forces and not only with the visible establishment of peaceful conditions.

Thus Nujoma set up his own series of new conditions which included not only the withdrawal of South African forces prior to the cessation of hostilities, and the repudiation of any monitoring of SWAPO bases outside Namibia, but also the demand for the establishment of five SWAPO military bases within Namibia. Upon the release later of minutes of the meeting in Luanda, Angola, it became apparent that both Nujoma and Angolan President Neto had decided to alter the nature of the settlement proposal, apparently fearing the prospects of democratic elections in Namibia. But by raising new terms for a settlement they attempted to shift the blame for any rupture of the negotiating process upon South Africa.

South Africa quickly and vigorously reacted in a letter of 14 February to Waldheim which denounced Nujoma for raising "a number of spurious objectives to parts of the proposal of the Five to which he had already committed SWAPO." South Africa charged him with "attempting to reopen negotiations on a non-negotiable settlement plan . . . to prevent the implementation of the settlement." as in a letter a week earlier South Africa emphasized that a cease-fire should take place not later than 20 February and that UNTAG forces should send advance units by the end of the month. Finally South Africa raised a vigorous protest over a major military assault by approximately 250 SWAPO personnel upon their base at Nkongo in South West Africa Namibia. With this major attack and the statements of Nujoma, South Africa posed the specific question to Waldheim whether SWAPO accepted the settlement proposal and had any intention to proceed with a cease-fire.

Waldheim in effect responded to the South African concerns at a press conference on 15 February. The Secretary General somewhat casually stated that "the acts of violence to which the Foreign Minister referred are not helpful in our effort." But at the same time Waldheim also seemed to question the entire negotiation process itself by asserting that "the basic issue here is that the South African Government is illegally in the Territory and this has to be stressed." In his formal reply to South Africa on 17 February. Waldheim repeated his statement on violence from the press conference. On other issues that had arisen he pledged that both Ahtisaari and himself would "pursue our efforts in order to secure the necessary clarification on those points."

South Africa reacted with dismay to the position of the Secretary General. After Waldheim's comment on the illegality of the South African role in Namibia, R. F. Botha responded that "the question arises as to whether we have anything further to say to one another." He also found "the description of the SWAPO attack as 'not helpful' to be inappropriately generous. The attack should be condemned for what it patently is, an artifice to undermine and prevent the implementation of the settlement." The increasingly tenous nature of the settlement became much clearer, and South African concerns more prophetic, with the issuance of the Waldheim report.

The Secretary-General's February Report

The new disagreements which began to surface in the various statements emerging from the Ahtisaari mission to South Africa and Namibia in January and the Front Line states and Nigeria in February ruptured into major disputes over the future role of the United Nations in Namibia with the appearance of General Waldheim's report on February 26, 1979.

In the opening section of his report Waldheim acknowledged the disagreements between the various parties to the negotiations. The report stated that:

during the meetings between my Special Representative and the representatives of South Africa and SWAPO, it became apparent that the two parties concerned had differing interpretations and perceptions regarding the implementation of certain provisions of the settlement proposal. With a view to resolving these differences, I considered it necessary to consult further with the five Western Powers, which had worked out the proposal with South Africa and SWAPO, as well as with the Front Line States. (3)

Waldheim's report then went on to assert that "In light of all the information I have been able to obtain, and after hearing the view of the parties directly concerned" he had decided to propose his resolution of the outstanding issues. But the report derived only from consultations with the five Western Powers and the Front Line states to the complete exclusion of South Africa, the authorities in Namibia and SWAPO, the main parties involved in the dispute. The new report, like the Secretary-General's report in September 1978, substantially altered basic understandings that South Africa had previously reached with the Western Powers. This, coupled with the lack of advance consultation on the contents, led Pretoria, with the support of the newly elected constituent assembly in Windhoek, to reject several key elements of the plan as unacceptable. Thus South Africa, having agreed to the U.N. plan and with Ahtisaari on his visit, found themselves in the invidious position of being obliged to reject the new report of the Secretary-General due to fundamental, last minute alterations in the plan.

The central dispute concerning the February report centered on the proposal to create SWAPO military bases in Namibia and the failure to provide any viable monitoring mechanism of SWAPO bases outside Namibia, principally in Zambia and Angola. The section of the February report on "Restriction to base" contained the following language:

Any SWAPO armed forces in Namibia at the time of the cease-fire will likewise be restricted to base at designated locations inside Namibia to be specified by the Special

Representative after necessary consultation. The monitored move of these SWAPO armed forces to base cannot be considered as a tactical move in terms of the cease-fire. (4)

Section 12 of the report provided that "All SWAPO armed forces in neighboring countries will . . . be restricted to base in these countries." However, the report notes that "the Proposal makes no specific provision for monitoring by UNTAG of SWAPO bases in neighboring countries." The report did urge the Front Line states to oversee this aspect of the proposal.

These provisions of the Waldheim proposal would allow any SWAPO military personnel in Namibia at the time of the declaration of a cease-fire to congregate with their arms at bases in the territory designated by the U.N.'s special representative. SWAPO has never been able to maintain any permanent bases in Namibia in the course of their protracted guerrilla war so these proposed bases would have to be newly created following the cease-fire. Possibly some bases being closed by South Africa would be used for SWAPO forces.

Throughout the war the only permanent bases of SWAPO have existed in various neighboring countries which have helped sustain their war effort against South Africa. As indicated in the Ahtisaari visit, South Africa emphasized the importance of monitoring potential military actions emanating from these bases as an integral element of a comprehensive peaceful agreement leading to elections. As mentioned above, Waldheim had agreed in his letter of January 1, 1979, that paragraph 12 of the April, 1978, agreement "is a very important element" and he expected the neighboring countries to allow UNTAG to monitor bases. But in the February proposal no specific agreement had been reached with the Front Line states to allow UNTAG officers to directly monitor SWAPO bases in their countries.

South Africa particularly denounced the proposal to establish SWAPO military bases in Namibia. In a speech to his Parliament, the South African Prime Minister protested that the April, 1978, agreement "contains no word, no reference whatsoever, to any possible establishment of bases for SWAPO troops who may fortuitously be in the territory at the date of the commencement of the implementation program." Moreover he noted that "At no time was there any mention or reference to this in any of the negotiating sessions" with the Five Western

Powers or direct discussions of South African officials with either Ahtisaari or Waldheim in January and February. The Prime Minister bluntly stated that "The five Western countries and Dr. Waldheim . . . must keep their word and carry out the agreement. That is the point. There is nothing more to discuss."

In its formal reply to the February report, South Africa reiterated that she had accepted the April, 1978 agreement "in its final and definitive form." Thus South Africa insisted that:

A. SWAPO armed personnel, like the South African forces, are to be restricted to existing bases. The restriction to base is to be monitored by UNTAG as is unambiguously provided for in the proposal and confirmed in your reply to me dated 1 January, 1979. This was also made clear to you in my letter of 20 February 1979.

B. SWAPO would have no right to create bases or be designated bases in South West Africa. The settlement proposal contains no provision directly or indirectly, either expressly or implied, that SWAPO forces who may accidentally or for a short duration be in the territory for the purpose of sabotage, are entitled suddenly to come forward on the day of the cease-fire with a claim to be assigned to camps which do not exist and in so doing achieve the establishment of bases in South West africa.

The Constituent Assembly in Windhoek adopted a resolution on March 5, 1979, objecting to various points in the February report. The resolution maintained:

(1) That there are no SWAPO bases inside South West Africa;

(2) That SWAPO armed forces which happen to be in South West Africa at the time that the cease-fire agreement takes effect, must return to their existing bases, in terms of the original proposal;

(3) That these bases, which are situated in the neighboring States, must be effectively monitored by UNTAG.

The resolution also reaffirmed that any new election be held not later than September 30, 1979, that all detainees in the Front Line states be able to return to Namibia and that no South African troops withdraw from Namibia without a complete cessation of hostilities. Mudge told the Assembly that "we are not prepared to be led by the nose any longer." He warned that without U.N. cooperation the Assembly would reconvene "to take a decisive decision which will not be renegotiable."

The two other political groups in Namibia who had refused to participate in the December election, and therefore had no representatives in the Constituent Assembly, also criticized the February proposal. Both the NNF and SWAPO-Democrats announced opposition to the creation of SWAPO bases in Namibia as being inconsistent with the principle of equality among the prospective competing political parties in Namibia. They argued that by only allowing one of the competing political groups in Namibia to have organized military forces and bases would destroy any fair competition among the various parties contesting U.N. supervised elections. The DTA similarly argued that if SWAPO were allowed military bases in Namibia then the DTA should also be allowed to create its own military forces and be granted bases. The spectre of numerous private armies in Namibia could easily forecast an impending civil war following any election outcome.

In an effort to deal with the failure of the February plan to provide some monitoring mechanism of SWAPO bases used for infiltration, the United States offered electronic sensoring devices to the United Nations forces for border surveillance. The U.S. also offered to obtain pledges from SWAPO and the Front-Line states to avoid any intimidation or other interference. The U.S. contended that sophisticated electronic monitoring devices could effectively detect any movement of men or materiel across the Namibian frontier and threaten a cease-fire. However, South African Foreign Affairs Minister Botha, after an investigation of the American proposal, said that his government could not accept the electronic devices under U.N. control as an effective substitute for on-site monitoring of SWAPO bases, but such devices could be a useful supplement in overseeing any cease-fire movements. South Africa also would not accept new verbal assurances from SWAPO and the Front-Line states as adequate security for Namibia.

Controversy over the Waldheim report:

South Africa's concern about the terms of the 26 February report exceeded any literal reading of the document as they suspected undue SWAPO influence in its drafting. South Africa claimed to have obtained an earlier draft copy of the report which bluntly set out the views of SWAPO which the final document consciously ignored. The fourth draft report, the authenticity of which the U.N. did not repudiate, noted, for example, that "The 2500 SWAPO armed forces would all be confined with all their arms and ammunition" to five bases inside Namibia.

The President of SWAPO made it clear that any effort to disarm the returning freedom fighters would be forcefully resisted. The declared objective of SWAPO was, that as South Africa withdrew its forces from Namibia, SWAPO would return its fighters from neighbouring countries into bases in Namibia, train them and eventually convert them into regular troops.

The intention of SWAPO to seize total power seemed fortified by another provision of the draft report which asserted that

The cease-fire which was to be declared simultaneously by South Africa and SWAPO should be considered binding only on South Africa within the three weeks following its declaration and not on SWAPO, since SWAPO would experience difficulties in transmitting passage of information on the cease-fire to all its freedom fighters in Namibia in time.

Thus it seemed that the final draft report substantially accommodated the various demands interjected into the settlement process by Neto and Nujoma in their meeting with Ahtisaari in Angola. Although going through numerous drafts, the Secretary-General never attempted to consult with South Africa about modalities of the settlement that only arose after the culmination of the Ahtisaari visit to Pretoria in early February. Given her exclusion from the dicussion process and the substantial alterations of the initial settlement proposal, the bitter South Africa reaction was predictable.

Composition of U.N. Forces

Beyond the major question of SWAPO bases and monitoring movements, the issue of the composition of U.N. forces used in Namibia also remained a source of dispute. Initially, it appeared that Waldheim would be able to choose the various nations to participate in the large peacekeeping force for Namibia as other U.N. forces had been chosen before, in a random worldwide selection of personnel from several presumably neutral countries. But as various countries were suggested objections arose from both SWAPO and South Africa.

The inclusion of Canadian forces in the draft proposal led to vigorous objections from Nujoma who bluntly warned "We don't want any NATO countries, such a force would be regarded as on the side of the enemy, and we would fight them." He only wanted African and Scandinavian countries who "showed sympathy with SWAPO." Shortly after this statement Nujoma narrowed his acceptability range still further. In an interview in a Kenyan newspaper, he said SWAPO objected to any participation of non-African countries in the U.N. force because "Namibia is an African problem."

Precisely the failure to include sufficient non-African countries not committed diplomatically to SWAPO raised objections by the South Africans. South Africa cited the "long-standing U.N. precedence, recognizing the views of the host country" as crucial in insuring confidence in Namibia that U.N. forces would not simply advance the cause of SWAPO. Thus South Africa stated, in its response to the February plan, that she "would not be willing to accept countries which had in the past identified themselves too closely and actively with the aims and activities of SWAPO. Such forces could not be expected to act with absolute impartiality." Apparently at the request of SWAPO, Waldheim omitted Canada from his proposed force, leading South Africa to object to the inclusion of any Warsaw Pact country.

South Africa certainly endured much greater risks in the creation of the UNTAG force than did SWAPO. With numerous unanimous votes in the United Nations over a period of several years nearly every country had officially recorded its opposition to South African administration of the territory and implicit support for the position of SWAPO. Nonetheless, SWAPO still felt it necessary to attempt to narrow the UNTAG force to various sympathetic African countries and thereby attempt to reap a more conspicuous psychological advantage from the U.N. presence during the elections.

The U.N. and South Africa

Even though bitterly disappointed with the Waldheim report, South Africa reluctantly agreed to continue talks with all the parties involved in the dispute in so-called proximity talks in New York on March 19, 1979. South Africa and the Internal Parties of Namibia proceeded to New York at the invitation of the U.N. to return to discussions on the original proposal, and not renegotiate it as they claimed the Waldheim plan effectively did. But upon arriving in New York they found that the U.N. session instead first took up charges leveled against South Africa by Angola for some air strikes against guerrilla targets. On 28 March the Security Council passed a resolution condemning "South Africa's utilization of the international territory of Namibia as a springboard for armed invasions and destabilization of the People's Republic of Angola." Angola, who had initiated the session to condemn South Africa refused to participate in discussions. But South Africa did consult with the Five Western nations and others in New York. No real progress seemed evident from the discussions and the South African representatives returned home, but emphasized that "this should not be seen as a setback as far as the talks are concerned, and should not be seen as the talks breaking down or anything to that effect."

In order to encourage acceptance of the new Waldheim proposals, the five Western powers sent representatives to Namibia at the end of March. They met with all political elements in Namibia and apparently hoped to at least persuade the groups who had boycotted the December elections that the U.N. plan offered a viable process towards the creation of an independent, democratic Namibia. But the effort failed to persuade the major dissenting party, the Namibian National Front. On April 2 they vigorously rejected the Waldheim report because the NNF remained "convinced that the failure to provide for monitoring by UNTAG of SWAPO bases in Angola and Zambia constitutes a deviation from the proposals and report endorsed by Security Council Resolution 435 (1978)." Secondly they contended that the creation of SWAPO military bases "will instill fear in the hearts and minds of the competing political parties and their supporters: and will be an undue influence and/or advantage in favour of SWAPO: such locations will therefore have a political impact: they will constitute a military and psychological advantage." (p.263b) Two weeks later the smaller SWAPO-Democrat group only conditionally accepted the arguments of the Western five. They demanded that retalitory action against SWAPO be mandated if the cease-fire breaks down. They also expressed the expectation that the implementation of the plan would lead to the release of "political prisoners on Robben Island and those who are held in detention camps in Angola and Zambia."

Meanwhile, frustrated by the actions of the United Nations, the Constituent Assembly elected in December assumed greater authority in Namibia and attempted to broaden its base of support. While specifically rejecting any "unilateral declaration of independence" as "not in the interest of South West Africa," a motion of the General Constituent Assembly on May 2, 1979 also maintained that continued negotiations "should not be permitted further to delay internal political, economic and social development." Thus even while endorsing continued negotiations, the Assembly also provided for the creation of a National Assembly consisting of the members of the existing Constituent Assembly and up to 15 other members, nominated from "bona fide democratic political parties which are not represented" at present. Moreover, the new Assembly was empowered to make laws with the consent of the Administrator-General and repeal or change all other laws, except those dealing with the Assembly itself. This provided real control over laws dealing with discriminatory practices.

South Africa acquiesced to the demands for increasing authority by the Constituent Assembly. Thus on May 21 the Constituent Assembly formally reconstituted itself as the new National Assembly. Joannes Skyrwer, told the new governmental body that "today it is South Africa that is prepared to grant us independence and the U.N. is trying to forestall it." (FBIS 5/23/79 p.E3). With the implementation of this plan together with the arrival in July of a new administrator General it seemed quite likely that the new National Assembly would take an increasingly vital role in the development of Namibia.

South Africa, in announcing the establishment of the National Assembly, stated "that this development in no way affects the status of South West Africa/Namibia." At the same time Pretoria reiterated her opposition to any "deviations from the Settlement Proposal" of April 1978 and indicated that the clarifications the five Western nations had attempted to make of these changes were not satisfactory.

The U.N. General Assembly took up the Namibia question

again on May 25. But no real debate took place as the General Assembly approved by a 96 to 19 vote, with 11 abstentions, a report of its Credentials Committee that South Africa should be denied the right to participate in the debate. The South African delegation walked out of the session and Western nations, who voted in the minority, deplored the actions of the U.N.

After refusing to allow South Africa to speak, the General Assembly proceeded to adopt another resolution on Namibia. This one reiterated points raised in most resolutions which had predated the movement toward a settlement the previous year. Thus the assembly ignored all other groups in Namibia by reaffirming its support for SWAPO as "the sole and authentic representative of the Namibian people." The Assembly called for "increased and sustained support and material, financial, military and other assistance" to SWAPO which "has direct responsibility for the Territory until independence." Finally the Assembly rejected any further discussions with South Africa by calling upon the Security Council to take action against South Africa which constituted "a serious threat to international peace and security." This resolution, (No. 33/206) passed by an overwhelming 119 to 0 margin, but the sixteen abstaining countries included all five Western nations involved in the negotiations. With three of these countries holding a veto power no action followed by the Security Council. The resolution had only a rhetorical impact.

South Africa, nonetheless, continued to indicate her willingness to renew negotiations with the U.N. As both an inducement for such negotiations or a fallback position if they utterly failed, Pretoria would continue to grant increasing sovereignty to Namibia, without ever officially proclaiming the government independent. Undoubtedly South Africa felt that her own negotiating position over Namibia had strengthened through a combination of effective local administration in Windhoek, a more sympathetic conservative government in London and the willingness of the U.S. Congress in Washington to override President Carter's policy on Rhodesia.

FOOTNOTES

(1) *South African Digest*, February 9, 1979, p. 1.
(2) *FBIS*, February 8, 1979, E1.
(3) Section 6 of U.N. Report S/13120.
(4) Section 11 of S/13120.

CHAPTER XI
NAMIBIA AND THE FUTURE OF SOUTHERN AFRICA

The developments in Namibia have profound implications for the future of the entire southern Africa region as well as for the security of the Western world. As indicated in preceding chapters, since the initial Western agreement with South Africa over granting independence to Namibia, protracted negotiations have involved seven other nations in the region. South Africa formally accepted the Western plan as modified by the U.N., but finally decided with reluctance to instigate further measures of self-government in Namibia on a unilateral basis because it felt obliged to reject provisions which would have provided bases for SWAPO armed forces within Namibia while failing to provide effective monitoring of SWAPO bases elsewhere.

Rhodesia and Namibia

Western participants in the negotiations over Namibia initially hailed the prospective settlement as a profound breakthrough in developments throughout southern Africa. Secretary of State Vance provided this assessment after Security Council approval of the Namibian resolutions in July 1978: "In my government's view, the importance of what has been achieved has implications which go far beyond the Namibian problem itself. The successful resolution of this international issue can encourage solutions for other pressing problems of Africa, particularly in the case of Rhodesia." Ambassador Young optimistically predicted there could be a peaceful settlement in Rhodesia "within the next few weeks" if a speedy solution with U.N. participation developed in Namibia.

In Senate debate in the summer of 1978 on lifting the economic sanctions against Rhodesia, Senator Clark, chairman of the African Affairs Subcommittee, cited the agreement on Namibia and stated that "we now stand on the threshold of turning around the course of events in southern Africa." He went on to argue that "What we are saying is that the Rhodesian Government need do more than what South Africa did in Namibia." (1)

Similarities do exist between the Namibia and Rhodesian situations and a constant interplay between developments in the two areas continues. However, the lessons of Namibia have been quite different from the superficial allusions of Vance, Young and Clark. The terms of settlement which the Western nations and the U.N. have attempted to impose upon Rhodesia has only a slight relationship to Namibia as the realities of the military-political situation in the two areas have constantly over-ridden any consistent application of abstract democratic principles.

Several very important resemblances exist between the situation in Namibia and Rhodesia. Both areas, long dominated by white minority rule have attempted to transfer power to tribally divided black majorities, yet at the same time retain some protection for the vital interests of the non-black population. In the process of transfering power, both countries have sought to gain international recognition, overcome sanctions imposed upon them by the United Nations and contend with the fierce regional hostilities led by the Front Line states who provide sanctuaries for guerrilla attacks. Elections held in Namibia in December, and in Rhodesia in April, successfully demonstrated popular support for the creation of multiracial governments and the advent of black rule under constitutional constraints.

In Namibia, South Africa maintains that she has largely worked within the framework of the requirements of the Western plan agreed to in April, 1975. But additional demands, such as for SWAPO military bases in Namibia, have prevented the completion of an agreement acceptable to the U.N. In Rhodesia, first the Smith government, and then its successor led by Bishop Muzorewa, contended that Salisbury has faithfully fulfilled the six requirements of the British to be recognized as a legal government. They also contended that by holding free and fair elections, and expressing a willingness to attend an all-parties conference, Rhodesia also fulfilled stipulations for lifting sanctions set under the Case-Javits amendment passed by the U.S. Congress.

However, despite these similarities, there are also significant differences between Rhodesia and Namibia. In Namibia the strength of South Africa and her determination to carry out a unilateral internal settlement if no other acceptable solution was possible, forced SWAPO forces to agree to resume negotiations on the Western plan in July 1978, a few days before South Africa had scheduled to announce its first steps towards implementing her own plan of settlement. The two other critical factors which forced SWAPO into an agreement were the pressures applied upon them by the front line states, particularly Angola, and internal divisions within SWAPO itself, although SWAPO only agreed to the U.N. plan after its rejection by South Africa.

Role of Angola

Angola, on the northern border of Namibia, has provided both a physical sanctuary and base of support for the SWAPO guerrilla forces operating in Namibia. This has prompted South African attacks which severely restrained guerrilla actions, especially as this same section of the country is also the principal locale of the continuing civil war in Angola.

Even with the assistance of upwards of 20,000 Cubans, over 1,000 East Germans, and massive logistical support from the Soviet Union, President Neto's regime has failed to consolidate its power in Angola. The nation still suffers from sporadic trouble on three military fronts. In the north, the Front for the Liberation of the Enclave of Cabinda has forced a reduction of oil production by 15 to 20 percent and constrained Angola's only significant source of foreign revenue needed to help sustain the Cubans and the war. Other Neto forces are tied down in the east in continued fighting with Holden Roberto's Front for the National Liberation of Angola. Neto has reached a partial accommodation with Zaire in order to curtail continued fighting in this area. But the major fighting has taken place in the south against U.N.I.T.A. (National Union for the Total Liberation of Angola) forces ably led by Jonas Savimbi. His forces control about one-third of the entire country. The Foreign Minister of the UNITA guerrilla army, Jorge Sangumba, has declared that "Angola will be the Soviet's Vietnam." Such a prediction necessarily depends upon outside support for their efforts such as the Soviets supplied to forces fighting the United States in Vietnam. Thus far, with only limited support, presumably coming from France and South Africa, the guerrilla forces have prevented Neto from consolidating control over much of the country. Even in the capital of Luanda, the government had to impose a curfew "To put an end to the climate of instability."

The three-front war and other disturbances have brought the economy of Angola to a halt. The country has reportedly accumulated a debt of over $1.3 billion to the Soviet Union and the cost of maintaining Cuban forces runs about $1.7 million a day. The generally desperate situation of Neto's regime has prompted his government to seek settlements with both Zaire and Namibia in order to attempt to isolate and eventually destroy the insurgent liberation movements in his country.

With Angola the major base of support for SWAPO, the decision of the Neto regime to pressure Nujoma into a settlement on Namibia has probably been critical. Without continued support for the resistance movements in Angola, Neto may have been willing to continue to use his nation as a base of support for the guerrilla attacks against South Africa in Namibia. Thus, limited intervention in Angola has undoubtedly played a vital role in bringing about a possible settlement in Namibia. Nonetheless, Andrew Young, often credited with taking a leading role in negotiations, publicly attacked France for her role in Angola, stating that France's "left hand may be destroying in Angola what its right hand builds in Zaire."

As we noted earlier, Angola refused to participate in the U.N. session on Namibia in March, 1979, but instead insisted upon a session condemning South African retaliatory strikes against guerrilla bases in Angola. Ironically, the obstruction by Angola of negotiations at that crucial point may eventually lead to the strengthening of forces attempting to undermine the Neto regime. The adoption of an internal settlement in Namibia, hostile to SWAPO, would mean continued support for the Angolan resistance movement which has inflicted severe casualties on not only Nujoma's forces, but also the MPLA and its Cuban allies.

Conclusion

South Africa has administered the territory of Namibia for over half a century. Despite the assertions that South African control over the territory was not legal, the United Nations and the major five Western nations negotiated with Pretoria to work out a general formula for a peaceful transition to independence. Only when the U.N., with the support of the Western nations, substantially altered the plan for independence did South Africa move forward independently with the December elections. As steps towards the full independence of Namibia, South Africa has granted increasing autonomy to regional authorities in Windhoek, particularly since the December elections.

South Africa welcomed international observers at the December elections, just as Rhodesia did at her elections four months later. Even with the conclusion of the December elections, and the vote for the DTA, South Africa continued to try to reach a broader accommodation with the U.N. and the Western powers for other elections including all parties to the conflict in Namibia. Thus, instead of simply rejecting the grant of independence and majority rule to Namibia, South Africa has proceeded to implement the terms of the initial April 25 Agreement with the five Western powers.

South Africa's concern over the potential creation of a hostile state on her northwestern frontier has undoubtedly figured prominently in her reluctance to come to any settlement that Pretoria believes unfairly favors the forces of the Marxist-oriented wing of SWAPO. Sam Nujoma, the leader of SWAPO, only very reluctantly gave tacit assent to any plan for the creation of a democratic form of government in Namibia. Given his general Marxist orientation, his past persecution of dissidents within his own organization, and his continued emphasis on violence as the road to power, Nujoma cannot be expected to adhere to any political process that does not effectively place his own forces in power.

Despite the present impasse on the problem of reaching international agreement on Namibia, formulas may yet develop that can accommodate all parties. Both South Africa and the leaders of the DTA who control the Constituent Assembly in Windhoek remain willing to work within the framework of the Western proposal on Namibia, and possibly even the Waldheim plan. But they have also declared their determination to pursue, if necessary, what they regard as a viable independent course of action which may precipitate a further measure of international censure, but which seems to offer better prospects of preventing the installation of a Marxist regime in Namibia. In order to succeed, South Africa and the DTA must effectively stave off other mounting external pressures and a continued low level internal resistance movement. It is possible that further elections which would include participation by both the

SWAPO-Democrats and the Namibia National Front, could consolidate internal support for the administration in Windhoek and even greater international support for an internal settlement in Namibia.

The development of a prosperous, democratic and racially harmonious society in Namibia would not only benefit the DTA, but also other political parties as well as the people of Namibia generally. More broadly such a development would greatly enhance South Africa's position in the region and reverse growing Soviet influence in the area. This, in turn, would then serve Western strategic interests in the area and provide access to critical raw materials.

The installation of a conservative government in Britain and the changing mood of the U.S. Congress concerning African policy are undoubtedly encouraging for Namibia. If the British (and possibly also the U.S. government) work out a settlement with the Muzorewa government in Rhodesia that does not compromise its position on the role of the guerrilla forces, then similar accommodations may be made in Namibia. The prevailing strength of South Africa provides Windhoek with a much greater capacity than Salisbury to resist pressures from Washington, London, or the Front Line states.

Nujoma effectively thwarted the settlement process for Namibia by raising new conditions in February, immediately following South Africa's acceptance of a framework for accommodation. Apparently frightened by the substantial DTA victory in the December elections, Nujoma sought to enhance his prospects of gaining power in Nambia through greater military strength during the transition period. Previously South Africa felt that the Western nations had failed to uphold the original April, 1978, proposal when the issue of Walvis Bay was injected in July, 1978, or when the Waldheim plan in September included a much larger U.N. force than previously agreed to. Issues of SWAPO dissidents and the composition of the UNTAG force also raised questions in South Africa about the actual implementation of the settlement proposals. Thus these clouds of uncertainty, gathering for almost a year created an atmosphere of distrust. Thus the additional alterations involving the creation of military bases in Namibia that SWAPO has never been able to maintain throughout the war, and the failure to monitor existing bases of SWAPO in the territories of her allies combined to force South Africa to demand a renewed adherence to the April 1978 proposal.

Finally, the previous negotiating positions of both Prime Minister Callaghan and President Carter were tilted in favor of the guerrilla forces in both Rhodesia and Namibia thereby effectively precluding any international settlement acceptable to those desirous of establishing moderate, democratic rule in both countries. The Western nations may in future decide to work within the framework of the new realities in the region. Even if they do not, South Africa will obviously play an increasingly influential role in a tacit alliance with both Rhodesia and Namibia. In either case, both Rhodesia and Namibia are now likely to emerge as independent states, better equipped, with Western or South African support or both, to cope with insurgent guerrilla movements. If that is the case, they may yet become a model of economic and political success for other developing African countries.

FOOTNOTES

(1) *Congressional Record*, July 26, 1978, S 11789-91.
(2) FBIS, July 27, 1978, E1

The Journal of Social and Political Studies is a quarterly publication dealing with topical issues in areas of social, political, economic, and international concern. Blending articles by outstanding academic authorities with those by administrative and executive leaders, the editors seek to provide an informative and stimulating analysis of circumstances affecting contemporary public policy issues.

===

JOURNAL OF SOCIAL AND POLITICAL STUDIES   ISSN 0362-580X
1716 New Hampshire Avenue N.W.
Washington D.C. 20009, U.S.A.

Dear Sir,

Kindly record a subscription in the following name. I enclose prepayment as checked below:

PLEASE PRINT OR TYPE

NAME ....
ADDRESS ....
....
....   (Zip) ....

===

AMOUNT ENCLOSED
(If subscription not placed through Subscription Agency)
===

INSTITUTIONS AND LIBRARIES:
    One Year $20.00   Three Years $55.00
INDIVIDUALS:
    One Year $10.00   Three Years $25.00

Publication: Quarterly (Spring, Summer, Fall, Winter). Size: 5"x9". Total pages per volume: 500 approx. Current Volume: No. 4 (1979). Standing Orders accepted. Subscriptions may be placed direct with the publisher at the address shown above or through Subscription Agents. Subscriptions accepted for complete Volume (calendar year) only